Professional Misconduct against Juveniles in Correctional Treatment Settings

Professional Misconduct against Juveniles in Correctional Treatment Settings

Lee Michael Johnson

AMSTERDAM • BOSTON • HEIDELBERG • LONDON
NEW YORK • OXFORD • PARIS • SAN DIEGO
SAN FRANCISCO • SINGAPORE • SYDNEY • TOKYO
ELSEVIER   Anderson Publishing is an imprint of Elsevier

Anderson Publishing is an imprint of Elsevier
The Boulevard, Langford Lane, Kidlington, Oxford, OX5 1GB, UK
225 Wyman Street, Waltham, MA 02451, USA

First published 2014

Notices
Knowledge and best practice in this field are constantly changing. As new research and experience broaden our understanding, changes in research methods, professional practices, or medical treatment may become necessary.

Practitioners and researchers must always rely on their own experience and knowledge in evaluating and using any information, methods, compounds, or experiments described herein. In using such information or methods they should be mindful of their own safety and the safety of others, including parties for whom they have a professional responsibility.

To the fullest extent of the law, neither the Publisher nor the authors, contributors, or editors, assume any liability for any injury and/or damage to persons or property as a matter of products liability, negligence or otherwise, or from any use or operation of any methods, products, instructions, or ideas contained in the material herein.

British Library Cataloguing in Publication Data
A catalogue record for this book is available from the British Library

Library of Congress Cataloging-in-Publication Data
A catalog record for this book is available from the Library of Congress

ISBN: 978-0-323-26452-5

For information on all Anderson publications
visit our website at store.elsevier.com

This book has been manufactured using Print On Demand technology. Each copy is produced to order and is limited to black ink. The online version of this book will show color figures where appropriate.

Working together
to grow libraries in
developing countries

www.elsevier.com • www.bookaid.org

DEDICATION

Dedicated to Tatyana

ABOUT THE AUTHOR

Lee "Mike" Johnson is Associate Professor of Criminology at the University of West Georgia. He received his Ph.D. in Sociology from Iowa State University in 2001. Professor Johnson's current research interests are in juvenile delinquency, victimization, and juvenile offender treatment. In the past he has published articles on the subjects of juvenile delinquency, victimization, corrections, and policing. His work appears in journals such as *Youth and Society*, *Journal of Social Psychology*, *Czech Sociological Review*, *Southwest Journal of Criminal Justice*, and *Policing: An International Journal of Police Strategies and Management*. He also edited a book, *Experiencing Corrections: From Practitioner to Professor* (Sage Publications). During the mid-1990s, Mike Johnson was employed as a youth worker in a residential treatment facility for behavior disordered and delinquent youth.

CONTENTS

A NOTE FROM THE SERIES CO-EDITOR

We are pleased to include *Professional Misconduct Against Juveniles in Correctional Treatment Settings* by Lee Michael Johnson in our new Real-World Criminology Monograph Series, which translates theory into practice.

Professional misconduct in correctional settings, including sexual exploitation, neglect, and physical abuse has long been a topic of concern and interest to corrections professionals as well as the public, especially concerning adult institutions. Movies, documentaries, and investigative journalists have focused on misconduct and related issues that, at times, have informed and educated the public on abuse and needed reforms. On other occasions, the media have promoted more simplistic, ratings-driven agendas that have misinformed the public and resulted in knee-jerk political policies and solutions.

While the traditional focus of corrections theory, policy, and practice tends to emphasize rehabilitation, deterrence, and public safety, Professor Johnson takes a close look at a somewhat neglected area of concern—professional misconduct against youth in correctional environments. He explores how different forms and expressions of misconduct not only traumatize juvenile victims, but also harm other correctional employees who genuinely care about maintaining high professional standards, as well the reputation of agencies charged with the custody and treatment of juvenile offenders.

Juveniles who are removed from deficient homes where they have experienced neglect, physical, and in some instances sexual abuse, and are remanded to correctional group homes and institutions where correctional staff violate professional boundaries and allow bullying and other forms of physical and psychological abuse to occur, are re-victimized by the very people who are charged with protecting and rehabilitating them. The results of such misconduct are too often a fast-track to more serious offending which can easily become a one-way bridge to adult incarceration.

In this monograph, Professor Johnson examines the nature and extent of professional misconduct against juvenile offenders and at-risk youth and offers some valuable practical solutions in addressing this too often neglected area of inquiry.

—**Michael Braswell**

CHAPTER 1

Introduction

In the search for improvements to the juvenile correctional system, much attention is given to the development of more effective approaches and techniques concerning rehabilitation, deterrence, and public safety. However, the pursuit of better corrections also involves the recognition and removal of barriers to achieving correctional goals that arise during daily practice. One such barrier is misconduct committed against juveniles by the persons employed to protect and help them. Obviously, misconduct interferes with the effective treatment of delinquent and at-risk youth, but it also harms the agency as a whole and creates a poor working environment for all employees.

In an earlier review of the literature, Powers, Mooney, and Nunno (1990) referred to institutional child maltreatment as a "national dilemma." Many children are placed in institutions because their home environments lack necessary care, safety, and treatment. If left in the home, they remain vulnerable to abuse and neglect. Settings such as long-term treatment facilities, foster and group homes, temporary shelters, and secure correctional facilities are operated to treat and protect youth, so it seems obvious that they would be preferable to troubled home environments. However, sometimes the opposite is true (Hobbs, Hobbs, & Wynne, 1999). Child custody institutions themselves carry the potential to place children at risk of maltreatment, as facilities are often isolated from public view and children in custody depend heavily upon the institution's employees to represent their interests (Powers, Mooney, & Nunno, 1990). Fortunately, the potential for institutional child maltreatment can be neutralized with effective policies and practices. Recognizing that juvenile corrections facilities carry the potential for institutional maltreatment is not the same as claiming that the system is, by nature, abusive and neglectful.

It is difficult to estimate just how often professional misconduct against juveniles occurs in correctional treatment settings. The available evidence does not suggest that it occurs very often, but neither does it suggest that it is very rare. Perhaps it is safe to claim that it happens far too often, and much more can be done to reduce it. Further, the severity of a problem behavior is not just determined by how often it occurs. The consequences of such behavior must also be assessed. As administrators realize, just one case of misconduct can cause major and extensive damage. Thus, while professional misconduct against youth does not appear to be an "epidemic," it continues to be a problem that requires better understanding and solutions.

1.1 CONSEQUENCES OF PROFESSIONAL MISCONDUCT AGAINST YOUTH

Professional misconduct against youth can bring about serious harm not only to program youth and their families, but to employees and agencies as well (Roush, 2008). The harm may extend further into the wider community, which may be affected by the future offending of troubled youth who received poor treatment, as well as by tax dollars spent by public agencies to recover from cases of misconduct. Since staff members are legally bound to protect residents' rights to safety and security, they play an important role in civil litigation involving harm done to youth. It takes a great deal of time, effort, money, and energy to manage an agency after an incident of serious employee misconduct, especially high profile cases (Roush, 2008). Lawsuits, tension, conflict, and overall bad morale create a poor treatment milieu and disrupt the delivery of services (Bloom, 1993).

The safety of youth is a primary responsibility of institutions that house or treat juvenile offenders. Child abuse in correctional facilities constitutes a failure by the juvenile justice system to protect youth (Davidson-Arad, 2005). That they have broken the law and some are violent themselves does not mean that these youths are less deserving of protection and safety than others. In fact, since many are also victims of crime (domestic abuse for example), they may be more vulnerable to the damaging effects of victimization; safety from harm will be essential to their healing and behavioral change (Davidson-Arad, 2005). Though they largely function and are viewed as punitive, secure juvenile correctional facilities are just as responsible for the protection of their residents as residential treatment centers, group homes, and institutional foster care.

Victimization by employees or peers undermines youths' chances of changing their thinking and behavior to become productive members of society. Thus, one of the possible long-term consequences of professional misconduct against youth is increased victimization in the community of institutionalized youth who received inadequate treatment. Many have histories of being abused and neglected, and the various forms of institutional victimization they experience likely exacerbate the psychological damage caused by earlier victimization (Davidson-Arad, 2005). Abusive behaviors on the part of employees, of course, directly bring harm to the youth, while neglect puts them in danger of harm (e.g. failing to protect children from assault or theft by peers and failing to attend to their health and hygiene needs). Failing to prevent youth-on-youth victimization does a disservice to both the victim and offender. An environment that tolerates bullying, for instance, can result in serious physical and psychological harm to victims, but it harms the perpetrators of bullying as well. If a child is allowed to bully, his or her orientation toward antisocial behavior is strengthened—the exact opposite of that which is intended by offender treatment (Browne & Falshaw, 1996).

Institutional re-victimization has particular implications for girls. Most system-involved girls have histories of victimization, often sexual. Acoca (1998, p. 562) writes "the abuses that a majority of girl offenders have experienced in their homes, in their schools, or on the streets are often mirrored and compounded by injuries they later receive within the juvenile justice system." These injuries may have a developmental impact beyond the girls themselves. If they are pregnant or have children, institutional maltreatment will also damage their capacity to raise their children to become healthy, productive, law-abiding citizens (Acoca, 1998).

As will be discussed later, many acts of misconduct represent a failure to maintain proper relationships with youth. Violating professional boundaries threatens harm to both the employee and the child. There might be some short-term gains; for example, youth may enjoy the attention given by over-involved staff or a distant staff member may avoid manipulation by youth, but boundary violations foster employee–youth relationships that inhibit effective treatment and management. A loss of objectivity and impaired judgment lead employees who are too close with or distant from youth in their care to make poor decisions. Employees with entangled boundaries may make youth increasingly dependent upon them and inhibit development of autonomy. Those with rigid boundaries may be less effective at building rapport with youth and instilling trust and a sense of self-worth in them (Davidson, 2004).

1.2 PURPOSE OF THE BOOK

This book covers current knowledge on 1) the nature of professional misconduct against youth, 2) its extent, 3) factors that increase its occurrence, and 4) solutions to the problem. Special emphasis is placed upon providing solutions to the problem. In fact, Chapter 5: Solutions is by far the largest chapter. Also, offered in the final chapter are suggestions for further study and action. The book is the result of an extensive review and analysis of recent literature on professional misconduct against institutionalized youth. To ensure quality, sources were restricted to peer-reviewed journal articles or book chapters, reputable professional periodicals, and official government reports. Further, the book explores the problem on a global level, drawing from studies conducted in multiple countries. Very little is published on professional misconduct in secure juvenile correctional facilities and residential or day treatment centers for delinquent youth. Thus, the analysis is extended to similar child placement settings such as shelters, group homes, and institutional foster care as they too often care for delinquent or at-risk youth. However, the information drawn from studies of related child care settings is used to address the problem of misconduct against youth placed in correctional settings specifically.

The book was largely written with the intention to provide assistance to current and future juvenile correctional staff, administrators, and practitioners, though it is hoped that it will reach a wider audience including political leaders, activists, and concerned citizens in general. Acknowledged in the book (especially in the final chapter) is that the problem cannot be solved without help from outside the agencies and organizations treating troubled youth—from child advocacy organizations to governmental leaders and the general public, for example. However, content throughout the book focuses mainly on information helpful to organizational policy and procedure as well as daily practice. In other words, it focuses mostly on what professionals working in the field can do to understand and solve the problem of professional misconduct against youth. Then again, the book does not serve as a training or "how to" manual. Rather, it is designed to fulfill its mission through educating students about the issue and provide a service to those in the field by consolidating knowledge available from a wide variety of qualified sources. The book is intended to help inform current and future professionals while allowing them to make their own judgments regarding anti-misconduct policies, procedures, and practice.

CHAPTER 2

The Nature of Misconduct

Defining professional misconduct against youth is important for policy and practice, not just for conceptual clarification. This includes defining particular types of misconduct. For example, the issue of what constitutes "abuse" has important implications for how to identify and respond to the abuse of children in placements (Kendrick, 1998). Professionals may be unsure about which acts by their colleagues constitute abuse and should be reported (Horwath, 2000). Child maltreatment in institutions can be similar to maltreatment that takes place in the home. It can take a variety of forms such as inadequate supervision, prolonged isolation, minor to very serious physical injury, involvement in sexual activities, violations of governmental regulations (denying home visits, for example), and inadequate treatment programs. However, with such a wide range of possibilities, professionals widely disagree over which acts constitute institutional child maltreatment and should therefore be reported to authorities and counted in incidence statistics (Powers, Mooney, & Nunno, 1990). Though difficult to develop, a valid definition of professional misconduct against juveniles in correctional treatment settings is needed for policy, practice, research, and theory.

2.1 PHILOSOPHICAL ISSUES

"Misconduct," specifically with respect to behavior committed by employees and volunteers working in juvenile correctional settings, should be defined and distinguished from related and conceptually overlapping offensive behaviors that take place in such settings. The meaning of the term is very subjective. It suggests different kinds of behaviors to different people and may vary according to one's position within or outside of an organization, goals/interests, political orientation, or analytic perspective. A useful, more neutral definition should be inclusive enough to cover the different forms of unethical and immoral behaviors that clearly threaten youth, yet exclusive enough to avoid convolution and too much conceptual repetition. While many of the behaviors constituting misconduct also fall under terms such as "rule breaking," "neglect," "abuse," and "crime," these are not terms synonymous with "misconduct." For the sake of focus this book specifically addresses misconduct committed by employees or volunteers against youth, though it is understood that other forms of misconduct are also harmful and interfere with an agency's efforts to treat youth.

Misconduct cannot be defined simply as the violation of institutional rules. First, "misconduct" conveys a sense of severity, and many rule violations are minor. Further, some rule violations do not intrinsically harm youth—they may defy administrative or supervisory preferences (strict dress codes for example). Thus, an objective definition of misconduct cannot be one that includes all behaviors deemed offensive by authorities. In fact, we must be careful to avoid a definition biased toward behavior committed by subordinate individuals. Misconduct can refer to behavior committed by higher status persons, including even CEOs and politicians (Skinner, 2003). Misconduct may also be committed by collective units such as departments and administrative units and exist in organizational practices. Asbridge (2007), for example, refers to a case in which it was discovered that a county juvenile detention center superintendent mishandled reports of sexual abuse from within his facility. Further, employee misconduct should not be an issue limited to residential environments, as misconduct can certainly occur in community correctional settings such as day treatment and probations. However, an objective definition of misconduct also cannot be one that includes all behaviors deemed offensive by those who challenge authority. Administrating on behalf of interests inconsistent with others' interests, including elite and self-interests, do not necessarily constitute misconduct. For example, an observer should not accuse administrators of misconduct *simply* because they employ a treatment mode not preferred by the observer.

Even if a clear, conceptually satisfying definition of misconduct can be established, decisions must still be made regarding sets of specific behaviors to which the definition may be applied. It will be easy to present some actions as misconduct. Physically aggressive behaviors, coercive and manipulative behaviors of a sexual nature, neglect of basic needs, verbal abuse, and theft, for example, provide clearer examples of misconduct. However, Groze (1990) refers to other forms of *inappropriate treatment* that are unique to institutional settings. These are "harm or threatened harm to a child's health or welfare which is caused by any violation of statutes, regulations, written rules, procedures, directives, or accepted professional standards and practices which is not otherwise classified to be abuse or neglect but which results in or creates the risk of injury to a child" (p. 231). These other possible forms of misconduct may require more explanation. The literature mentions several other forms of harmful behaviors which also may be considered professional misconduct against youth.

Recent literature often cites Gil's (1982, cited in Kendrick, 1998) institutional abuse typology: 1) physical and sexual, 2) program, and 3) system. Physical and sexual abuse involve actions which could occur in family situations, except they are perpetrated by a professional caregiver. Program abuse occurs when programming does not meet acceptable standards, policies are extreme or unfair, and child guidance techniques are harsh, inhumane, or unusual. Program abuse includes over-medication (using medication to control youth), unwarranted use of restraint and isolation, and harsh discipline. Isolation in control rooms or "pin-down units" may resemble conditions of "solitary confinement" in adult prisons. System abuse is the most difficult type to define, identify, and correct, perhaps because it involves multiple agencies. Large, complicated childcare systems with very limited resources are incapable of guaranteeing proper care to all children. System abuse may be more identifiable by its result—primarily that some children "drift" through several placements, which denies them the stability and continuity needed to develop (Gil, 1982, cited in Kendrick, 1998). By the time they leave care, system-abused youth will be ill prepared to function in mainstream society, lacking educational qualifications and employment and housing opportunities, for example (Kendrick, 1998).

Gil's typology, especially in terms of system abuse, suggests that definitions of misconduct—assuming that some forms of maltreatment can be considered misconduct—cannot be restricted to isolated individual action and frontline staff behavior. Lerman (1994) points out that some legal definitions of abuse and neglect include the initial or continued placement of children into facilities and programs inappropriate to their needs with knowledge that such placements can harm the child. Applying this kind of definition, juvenile courts that fail to place adjudicated youth in "the least restrictive alternative" (e.g. overusing incarceration which is supposed to be a "last resort alternative") may be accused of child maltreatment. Thus, it is possible for powerful actors such as judges and child welfare authorities to commit maltreatment.

However, the purpose here is to define "misconduct." Abuse, neglect, and maltreatment are not terms synonymous with misconduct. When professionals directly abuse or neglect youth, they are indeed engaging in behavioral misconduct. But are all forms of maltreatment "misconduct"? Abusive and neglectful conditions are not always traceable to the abusive and neglectful actions of individual or group actors. Definitions of the term misconduct may vary but it is probably safe to say that it generally refers to distinct intentional decisions and behaviors enacted with either ill regard or disregard for rules, laws, or ethical principles that protect the welfare of others. It is possible that some of the unacceptable conditions experienced by youth in placement are not due to intentional harmful actions. In fact, many if not most administrators and staff who run or work in problem facilities are probably well-meaning and give their best effort. Larger social systems are often responsible for the maltreatment of youth, which is just as bad a problem as individual level maltreatment, but claiming that "the system" engages in misconduct would be committing a reification error. One cannot speak of an abstract social system as if it were as concrete as a human individual or small group. Thus, to make a good argument that pervasive conditions experienced by youth are due to professional misconduct, one should identify the exact decisions and/or actions of individuals acting alone or in concert with others that violate protections for youth. One should not assume that the existence of these conditions means that they are caused by misconduct on the part of employees or professionals working with the youth service agency. However, as explained later, poor conditions that may be due to political, economic, and cultural forces operating beyond the control of agencies do make individual or group misconduct more likely to occur.

2.2 ABUSE, NEGLECT, AND POOR ROLE MODELING

A major form of professional misconduct against youth is sexually offensive behavior. Roush (2008) argues that staff sexual misconduct should be defined as a continuum of inappropriate behaviors, ranging, for instance, from serious crimes to foul language. Such a definitional approach is useful in that it recognizes not only severe acts such as physical sexual assault, but also those that may be less severe—more unprofessional than criminal—yet still harmful. For example, telling a sexually inappropriate joke to another employee in front of a child, even one that seems only slightly risqué, would constitute sexual misconduct with youth. Such an act would usually be less harmful than a physical assault and may not even be directed toward the child, but it can cause significant harm. The joke could emotionally disturb the child, one who has been sexually victimized for instance. Also, a child with sexual offending issues could interpret the joke as an affirmation of one's own sexually inappropriate attitudes (thereby interfering with treatment). Other forms of misconduct should also accommodate a wide enough range of behaviors. For example, non-sexual violence can also range from bodily physical assaults to aggressive verbal statements.

Professional misconduct against youth, then, includes a variety of unprofessional and unethical behaviors that negatively impact youth. These include inappropriate attire, profanity and other crude language, and disrespecting youths' privacy (Roush, 2008). Establishing clothing that is inappropriate to wear around youth is difficult and controversial—subject to many different opinions—but some types are clearly problematic. Clothing that displays sexual or violent imagery (such as some novelty T-shirts), for example, clearly sends the wrong message to youth and could upset those with victimization issues. Profanity may often seem to be innocent, especially if accidental, or even a means by which to relate to youth. However, profanity is very risky, as it is often another form of violent and/or sexual expression and blurs the lines of professionalism. Further, when employees use profanity around youth, they may send the message that it is okay to behave inappropriately. Youth workers serve as role models for youth; how they dress and what they say have important implications for youths' treatment and their behavior in the setting. Privacy violations include: failing to announce when entering a youth's room, reading personal mail or other written materials (when not necessary for security), unnecessary/excessive monitoring of showers and toilet areas, and group strip searches (Roush, 2008). These can be greatly traumatic to youth and are often violently or sexually suggestive even if it is not the intention of the youth worker.

Empirical research may help determine misconduct behaviors. Freundlich, Avery, and Padgett's (2007) qualitative study on New York

City congregate care facilities (including group homes and residential treatment centers) revealed "inappropriate staff conduct" as an important threat to residents' safety. Professionals interviewed in the study identified corporal punishment, use of restraints, inappropriate isolation, deprivation, bullying of children, strip searches, and anal cavity checks as forms of inappropriate staff conduct. Young adults formerly in congregate care also identified inappropriate restraint (as punishment instead of security) and isolation (to one's room, or another small room, for excessively long periods) as staff threats to youth safety. They also identified physical abuse and violence (a case of beating and a case of attempted strangling were alleged); sexual abuse; verbal abuse and intimidation (threatening or implying assaults); provoking hostility; providing drugs; failure to protect and maintain control; failure to prevent theft of property; exposure to sexual relations among staff members; lack of supervision; and indifference to the presence of safety threats (e.g. poor physical conditions and potential attacks by peers and other staff members) (Freundlich et al., 2007).

Another dimension to add to the conceptualization of professional misconduct against youth is that it is a violation of international human rights. The United Nations established several human rights principles for juvenile justice in the 1980s (Kiessl & Würger, 2002). Particularly significant are the United Nations Convention on the Rights of the Child and Rules for the Protection of Juveniles Deprived of their Liberty. The UN set international minimum standards for the treatment of children in conflict with the law. Here, the UN emphasized the well-being of the child and his/her family and the need to develop conditions ensuring that children are able to pursue a meaningful life in the community. The standards are intended to cover all aspects of a juvenile justice system including training of personnel and conditions of facilities. Punishment beyond the necessary deprivation of liberty is prohibited, meaning that any form of abuse or neglect cannot be part of responses to delinquency or other problem youth behavior. In fact, the standards dictate that safeguards be instituted to prevent further harm to the physical or psychological well-being of incarcerated youth (Kiessl & Würger, 2002).

As part of a 1998 National Council on Crime and Delinquency (NCCD) study, Acoca and colleagues conducted structured qualitative interviews with a convenience sample of 193 girl offenders in four counties in the state of California (Acoca, 1998). A majority of the interviews took place in juvenile hall settings. Institutional maltreatment was not an intended focus of the study, nor was it represented as a question in the instrument. However, many girls reported emotional, physical, and sexual abuse as well as poor environmental conditions while being detained. Further, interviewers directly witnessed some abusive conditions themselves. Acoca (1998) points out that whether these abuses are due to inappropriate interactions between professionals and girls, procedural practice, or environmental conditions, they are all violations of specific international agreements and standards governing the rights of juveniles deprived of freedom (e.g. United Nations Convention on the Rights of the Child and Rules for the Protection of Juveniles Deprived of their Liberty).

The most common *emotional abuse* reported by girls in the NCCD study include name calling, swearing/foul language, shouting, threats of and actual isolation (in their room or an isolation room), threats of physical harm/intimidation. Name calling included sexually demeaning names, which are especially harmful to sexual abuse victims' already fragile sense of self-worth. Also reported were males watching during strip searches, sexual touching and advances by males, and physical and procedural threats of retaliation if girls report abuse (e.g. using mace and interfering with court dates). Girls reported a variety of *physical and sexual abuses*. Some pregnant girls reported being handcuffed or otherwise restrained, making them fearful that they would fall on their stomachs. One girl reported overuse of strip/visual body cavity searches, male staff viewing and making demeaning comments to girls in the shower, and staff threatening (e.g. to withhold food) girls to prevent them from filing grievances. Strip search abuses seemed to be a common practice. NCCD researchers themselves observed girls being strip searched and physically examined in the presence of males. Also reported were incidents of a girl being slammed against a wall and a room search in which a girl's Bible was torn (Acoca, 1998).

Girls in the NCCD study also reported unhealthy environmental conditions. One was poor food quality. Though it is unreasonable to expect institutions to serve fancy food, they must serve food that meets nutritional standards and is prepared and distributed in a clean, safe manner. This is especially important considering that most system-involved youth come from low-income backgrounds and are thus at

higher risk of poor nutrition. One girl reported unclean fruits and vegetables, and a researcher who ate lunch with a group of girls reported
that the vegetables smelled and tasted rotten. One pregnant girl worried that she was not getting enough food for her baby because of the
long time between dinner (4:30–5:00 pm) and breakfast. Another poor
condition was dirty linens (sheets, washcloths, and towels) as well as
clothing, which also often did not fit. This creates obvious sanitary
problems. In fact, several girls reported widespread head lice and sca-
bies. Also, facility overcrowding combined with a lack of ventilation,
fresh air, and sunlight promotes risk of airborne diseases such as tuber-
culosis (a larger problem among disadvantaged populations). Another
sanitary problem was insufficient access to hygiene products. For
example, girls typically had to ask for one sanitary napkin at a time
rather than being given a complete supply right away. Finally, girls
may not have been provided with adequate exercise. Some girls com-
plained that they did not have the same access to outdoor and recrea-
tional activities as boys; some said that they were not allowed to go
outside to play sports, such as basketball, at all (Acoca, 1998).

Misconduct includes tolerating victimization of youth by others—
by other employees, peers, and family members, for example. In addition to being responsible for their own behavior, persons who work
with children bear much of the responsibility for the behaviors of
others, especially children in their charge. Further, they are responsible
for being attuned to children's situations and becoming aware of and
acknowledging their victimization and threats to their safety
(Davidson-Arad, 2005). Failing to take adequate action in protecting a
youth's person and property, including efforts to maintain ignorance
of victimization or threats, constitutes a form of neglect. One example
is failing to take youth-on-youth bullying seriously. Bullying results in
serious harm to its victims and interferes with the treatment of offenders, but employees with lax attitudes toward bullying often fail to prevent it from occurring (Browne & Falshaw, 1996).

Browne and Falshaw (1996) investigated one secure residential center in the United Kingdom and found that, of 25 residents at one point
in time, 56% "were at risk of bullying their peers" (p. 124). They also
found that, of 44 youths treated at the center over a six-month period,
47% "regularly bullied their peers on the secure units and 56% were
frequent victims of bullying behavior" (p. 124). Since employees are

responsible for the physical and emotional safety of youth in residential care, it is their duty to prevent bullying among the youth in their charge. They must also properly respond to bullying when it occurs. Browne and Falshaw (1996, pp. 126–127) recommend that personnel "show support for the recognition of the victim's experiences" and "demonstrate work is being carried out with the bully." For the bully, they should "demonstrate support for the victim and develop the individual's understanding and empathy for others."

It seems reasonable then to view the tolerance of peer abuse as misconduct. Interactions between employees and youth may determine a variety of types of harm done to youth. In some cases staff may encourage, not just tolerate, attacks on youth, thereby making them accomplices in abuse. Peterson-Badali and Koegl (2002) found evidence that in addition to ignoring peer violence, juvenile correctional guards sometimes actively encourage assaults and rumor spreading, through incentives or implicit requests, as a means of indirect control.

2.3 INAPPROPRIATE RELATIONSHIPS

Assaults against youth are clearer cases of misconduct, but misconduct that results from consensual or strict interactions with youth may be more difficult to identify. Professional misconduct is not necessarily explicit aggressive behavior committed with ill intent. Some troublesome questions must be asked. Can developing close relationships with youth lead to misconduct? Can expressions of good will toward youth cause them harm at times? Can one be "too professional" (rigid) with youth? Youth care workers are faced with the difficult task of balancing personal and communal needs to care for and bond with youth with personal and communal needs to maintain professional distances from them. Regardless, professional relationship boundaries between workers and youth must be maintained.

Identifying interpersonal boundary violations in practice is very difficult, as many situations will fall into the "gray area" of boundaries (Davidson, 2004). Judgments of certain relationships and interactions vary widely among different individuals and agencies. Some situations may have both advantages and disadvantages that make it difficult to determine their level of appropriateness. There can also be several situational contingencies to consider, such as the needs of the child, the role of the employee, the quality and depth of the employee–child relationship, the physical environment, the size of the community, and cultural context (Davidson, 2004). Obviously, romantic relationships are completely unacceptable, but what about developing friendships or kinship-type relationships? Being friendly helps build rapport, and "quasi-parenting" may offer the nurturance and discipline that many youth are lacking. However, behaving as a child's peer will undermine one's authority and informally "adopting" a child can lead to favoritism, irrational decision-making, and unrealistic expectations by the child. The youth worker may be fulfilling a personal need to nurture, to be important to someone. Thus, it is conceivable that "getting too close" with youth constitutes misconduct. Davidson (2004) mentions several specific experiences and behaviors that may indicate entangled boundaries. These include unrestrainedly revealing personal information, becoming unusually invested in changing a child's behavior, becoming extremely upset with a child's choices, spending an unusually large amount of time with a child, and exchanging gifts.

Then again, it is also conceivable that maintaining distant relationships fosters misconduct. Failing to show signs of emotional support demonstrates rigid boundaries that stand in the way of productive employee–child relations (Davidson, 2004). Youth care workers commit emotional neglect when they do not offer needed, emotionally supportive stimuli. Needed stimuli are praise for accomplishments and proper behavior, encouragement to achieve goals, reassurances that the child is a valuable person, attentive listening, consolation upon experiencing traumatic events or conditions, and sharing humor. Child care employees are institutionally and legally responsible for meeting all of the child's basic needs; engaging in any form of maltreatment toward a child, abusive or neglectful, would constitute misconduct. Of course, it would be unreasonable to argue that employees must be affectionate toward children in the same manner as a parent, for example. However, if they are incapable of showing basic warmth and regard then they are extremely limited in their ability to administer preventative and rehabilitative treatment. Davidson (2004) mentions several specific experiences and behaviors that may indicate rigid boundaries, including not caring about a child, loathing going to work, being unjustifiably pessimistic at work, exhibiting no emotion, and minimizing the degree of pain felt by a child.

Sexual Misconduct

    Rape/Sexual Assaults (forced intercourse or oral sex)

    Non-Penetrative Acts (e.g. kissing, heavy petting) Obtained with Threat or Manipulation

    Consensual Sexual Relationships with Youth

    Romantic Relationships with Youth without Physical Contact

    Sexual Touching/Physical Harassment (e.g. groping, inappropriate hugs and pats)

    Verbal Sexual Statements/Harassment (inviting or gratifying sexually explicit comments)

    Indecent Exposure (exposing private body parts, in whole or in part)

    Violating Sexual Privacy/Voyeurism (e.g. unwarranted shower checks, body searches)

Nonsexual Abuse

    Assault and Battery (e.g. hitting, kicking, slapping, pushing, poking, for any reason)

    Overuse/Misuse of Physical Restraint (e.g. manual holds, medication, straps)

    Overuse/Misuse of Confinement (e.g. in youth's room or separate control room)

    Providing Youth with Illegal Substances (directly or allowing/facilitating access)

    Non-Verbal Intimidation/Posturing (e.g. getting too close, glaring, violent gestures)

    Provoking Youth into Misbehavior (any act to make youth angry, upset or frightened)

    Encouraging Any Kind of Assault by Peers (e.g. through suggestion or rewards)

    Verbal/Psychological Abuse (e.g. shouting, swearing, putting down/insulting)

    Creating Dangerous Environment (e.g. physical hazards, using substances, rough play)

    Labor (exploitive or excessively punitive/demeaning use of work by youth)

    Violating Nonsexual Privacy (e.g. unnecessary room search, reading personal materials)

    Verbal Threats of Harm (of any kind)

Neglect

    Failure to Meet Basic Needs (e.g. food, medical, exercise, hygiene, emotional support)

    Failure to Protect from Physical Harm (e.g. from self, peers, visitors, other staff)

    Failure to Intervene in Verbal Attacks or Intimidation (same as above)

    Lack of Supervision (e.g. leaving youth by themselves or not paying attention to them)

    Favoritism (meeting some youths' needs over others')

    Interference with Treatment (e.g. blocking access to therapeutic activities)

Property Offenses

    Theft of Youths' Property (anything belonging to youth)

    Theft of Youth-Intended Agency Property (gifts, supplies, donations)

    Overconsumption/Use of Shared Resources (e.g. food, use of recreational facilities)

    Damaging Youth Property (anything belonging to youth)

Figure 2.1 Types of professional misconduct against youth.

Duplicity

 Falsifying Records (e.g. changing or destroying completed reports, false statistics)

 Making False Reports (e.g. giving false accounts on incident reports or shift logs)

 Bearing False Witness (e.g. lying about youths' behavior or covering for colleagues)

 Misrepresentation of Facts (e.g. de-contextualizing or placing in an improper context)

 Trickery (e.g. false promises of rewards or punishments to youth, misleading colleagues)

Unprofessionalism/Poor Role Modeling

 Improper Language (e.g. swearing around youth)

 Inappropriate dress (crude imagery, too informal, dirty, damaged, somewhat revealing)

 Fraternizing with Youth (treating youth as peers rather than their authority)

 Overexposure to Personal Relationships (e.g. romantic, particularly with other staff)

 Unusual Investment in Youth (e.g. excessive gifts, admonishment for misbehavior)

 Pessimism (e.g. negative comments about the agency, treatment, or "life" around youth)

 Laziness (e.g. being excessively sedentary, refusing to take youth to group activities)

Figure 2.1 (Continued).

2.4 CONCLUSION

Based on the literature covered in this chapter, professional misconduct against youth as it applies to juvenile offender treatment workplaces (secure, non-secure residential, or community settings) may be abstractly defined as: decisions and behaviors enacted by individuals, alone or in concert with others, with either ill regard for, disregard for, or inadequate consideration of rules, laws, practices, or ethical principles that protect the welfare and rights of juveniles and children. "Individuals" here refers to any adult working in an official capacity with troubled juveniles: employees (from frontline staff to the highest administrator), contracted practitioners (e.g. specialized therapists), public officials (e.g. family and child service workers, probation officers, and judges), interns and practicum students, and volunteers. Also, it should be noted that the definition does not require that an action must actually result in harm. Misconduct need only create the risk of harm (actions made without proper regard for others by nature usually do so). To elaborate further and perhaps provide a useful analytical framework, a categorization of specific types of misconduct is offered in Figure 2.1.

CHAPTER 3

The Extent of Misconduct

Though a difficult task, the extent of professional misconduct against youth must be assessed if the true magnitude of the problem is to be understood. Estimates of the extent of misconduct must be viewed in the context of the relative seriousness and frequency of different types of acts. Care must be taken to avoid blowing the problem out of proportion. For example, sexual abuse, physical assault, denial of needs, and failure to protect (from other youth) are a few of the very serious forms of misconduct against system-involved youth which have been reported. But are they typical forms of misconduct? Perhaps milder forms of misconduct (verbal abuse, petty theft, inactivity with the residents, etc.) occur more often. Groze (1990) found that inappropriate treatment (violations of statutes, regulations, rules, procedures, directives, or professional standards and practices) was reported and confirmed more often than physical abuse, sexual abuse, and neglect at juvenile institutions in one southwestern state in the US.

Professional misconduct against youth is undoubtedly a very serious issue, and no amount of it should be tolerated. However, does it warrant as much concern as that given to other problems in care institutions such as school violence, medical malpractice, and maltreatment in nursing homes? Referring to one particular type of misconduct, one juvenile detention center superintendent stated in a *Corrections Today* article that: "Sexual assault—both youth-on-youth and staff-on-youth—in juvenile correctional settings is a problem that cannot be ignored" (Asbridge, 2007, p. 80). However, little is published on professional misconduct against youth in placements, implying that the issue is not widely viewed as a major problem. Still, reasons to suspect that the problem might be large enough for more concern can be found in the literature.

Bloom (1993) argued that abuse in the residential care of children is a serious problem that lacks proper attention. He charged that statements made in the literature indicating that these cases of abuse are uncommon were not backed by empirical research and suggested that the oversight may not be accidental. Reports of abuse will often be received as threats to the reputation and functioning of an institution, thus an administration may be reluctant to validate the reports even if they are true. The tendency toward institutional self-defense makes it more difficult to prevent, detect, and expose incidents of staff abuse. To help explain his skepticism, Bloom (1993) cited firsthand knowledge of nine staff members who sexually abused twelve children during the 1980s, and stated that it is unlikely that his experience was unique. Bloom gives good reasons to scrutinize claims minimizing the seriousness of employee misconduct in residential youth care and makes a passionate plea to consider that such incidents may be fairly common. However, most of the evidence he offers, though valuable, is anecdotal and thus improper for broader generalization. Further, he does not specify the inclusion of facilities housing juvenile offenders in "residential care." His analysis possibly targets foster care centers and mental health facilities that do not specialize in the care and treatment of offenders. Still, residential facilities housing juvenile offenders are indeed responsible for the care of children and the organizational circumstances and characteristics identified in Bloom's (1993) arguments may be found in juvenile correctional settings.

3.1 A LOCAL PROBLEM

In their study of congregate care in New York City, Freundlich, Avery, and Padgett (2007) found that "stakeholders" (individuals, groups, and organizations working closely with and/or directly affected by residential care delivery) were worried about the safety of youth in the city's foster care system. Interviews with family court judges, children's attorneys, social workers, representatives of child advocacy groups and private child welfare agencies, and formerly placed youth showed that many found inappropriate/aggressive staff behavior and poor physical conditions to be among serious threats to safety in congregate care (Freundlich et al., 2007). Also, in a study of secure juvenile correctional facilities in Ontario, Canada, Peterson-Badali and Koegl (2002) found that physical safety, fighting, and general security issues were among the major concerns of youth in custody.

As stated earlier, tolerating or encouraging peer offending is a form of misconduct. While incidents of employee-on-youth violence may be relatively infrequent, peer-on-peer violence is fairly common in custodial settings. Peterson-Badali and Koegl (2002) examined the role of correctional staff in peer violence using retrospective accounts of youth who spent time in secure custody in Ontario, Canada. One hundred youths in custody were interviewed (semi-structured) about their experiences in former placements, representing a total of fourteen institutions. The researchers coded the qualitative data and computed frequencies, including the following: About 17% did not feel protected by staff and almost 15% indicated that they did not always feel protected. Twenty-six percent claimed that staff used too much force on them and about 53% claimed to witness staff using too much force on another resident. About 46% claimed that staff ignored possible trouble and about 47% claimed that staff somehow induced peer violence. About 16% reported personally intimidating a peer and about 17% reported personally assaulting a peer in response to inducements from staff (only about 2% reported rumor spreading). About 10% reported witnessing peer intimidation and about 22% reported peer assault in response to inducements from staff (only about 4% reported rumor spreading). About 10% claimed that staff allowed (not induced) peers to spread rumors about a resident and only about 4% claimed that staff allowed peer intimidation and assault. Also, about one-third heard jokes or hints that a resident should be harmed but were not sure that they were invitations to action, and about one-third heard such jokes or hints and *did* interpret them as an invitation to action. Peterson-Badali and Koegl (2002) acknowledge that these frequencies are relatively low and youth reports carry the potential for exaggeration. However, they reason that some amount of the allegations is likely to be true, this amount is nontrivial, and any amount of staff violence against youth and staff-induced peer violence is problematic from a clinical and policy standpoint.

Hobbs, Hobbs, and Wynne (1999) studied cases of abuse in foster and residential care in Leeds, England. Examined were pediatrician reports of abuse that happened to children while under foster or residential care during 1990–1995. Among 133 children, 158 incidents of abuse were identified. During the time of the study, there were 178 children placed in residential care and there were 34 incidents of abuse among 25 children assessed: twelve were abused physically, six were abused sexually, and six experienced both. Of these, eight children were abused by a staff member. Compared to the general city population rate, children in residential care were six times more likely to have been assessed by a pediatrician for abuse (foster children were seven to eight times more likely). Thus,

Hobbs, Hobbs, and Wynne (1999) concluded that children in foster and residential care are a group at risk for maltreatment.

3.2 A NATIONAL PROBLEM

Concerned caregivers and advocates, small studies, and well-formed position papers can be persuasive in establishing that professional misconduct against youth involves serious harmful offenses and is a problem that needs better solutions. They also suggest that the conditions that facilitate misconduct may widely exist. Still, they do not establish that it indeed occurs frequently. Thus, it is important to review research estimating national rates of professional misconduct against youth. Unfortunately, such research is rare. National level research is usually conducted by governmental authorities and tends to be restricted to physical and sexual assault. Because these studies focus on a few severe types of misconduct, they tend to suggest that severe abuse occurs rather infrequently. To provide an example, research in the United States is covered here. Recently, US Department of Justice programs have conducted projects that include the collection of data on employee abuse of juveniles in correctional treatment facilities.

The Prison Rape Elimination Act of 2003 required the Bureau of Justice Statistics (BJS) to "develop new national data collections on the incidence and prevalence of sexual violence within correctional facilities" (Beck & Hughes, 2005, p. 1). The BJS now conducts annual national surveys of administrative records on incidents of sexual violence reported to authorities in public and private correctional facilities. The first survey collected data on reports made in 2004. The sample of 2,700 correctional facilities (holding 79% of all adults and juveniles in custody) included 807 juvenile facilities (510 state, 228 private, and 69 local) covering a population of 62,935 (41,196 state and 21,739 local/private). All state correctional systems in the U.S. were selected for the survey, while private and local facilities were sampled.

In addition to inmate-on-inmate offenses, *staff sexual misconduct* and *staff sexual harassment* were included as measures of sexual violence and defined based on National Institute of Corrections definitions. *Staff sexual misconduct* was defined as "any behavior or act of a sexual nature [consensual or nonconsensual] directed toward an inmate by an employee, volunteer, official visitor, or agency representative," including "romantic relationships between staff and inmates" (Beck & Hughes, 2005, p. 3). Specific acts include intentional touching of genitals or other erogenous zones "with the intent to abuse, arouse, or gratify sexual desire;" uncompleted attempts (through threat or request) at sex acts; and "indecent exposure, invasion of privacy, or staff voyeurism for sexual gratification" (Beck & Hughes, 2005, p. 3). *Staff sexual harassment* was defined as "repeated verbal statements or comments of a sexual nature to an inmate by employee, volunteer, official visitor, or agency representative, including: demeaning references to gender or derogatory comments about body or clothing; or profane or obscene language or gestures" (Beck & Hughes, 2005, p. 3).

Juvenile facilities reported the highest rates of alleged staff sexual *misconduct* in the 2004 study (Beck & Hughes, 2005). The rate for state juvenile facilities was 11.34 per 1,000 youth (467 incidents reported nationally). Even the smaller rate for private/local juvenile facilities, 3.22 per 1,000 youth (70 incidents reported in the sample), was nearly three times the rate of that for state and federal (adult) prisons. Juvenile facilities also reported the highest rates of alleged staff sexual *harassment*. The rate for state juvenile facilities was 1.34 per 1,000 youth (55 incidents reported nationally) and the rate for private/local juvenile facilities was 2.21 per 1,000 youth (48 incidents reported in the sample). In comparison, the rates of alleged sexual harassment for the different types of adult facilities varied from only 0.26 to 0.51 per 1,000 inmates. With 62,935 youth in custody and 537 total allegations made in state and private/local facilities in 2004 (Beck & Hughes, 2005), the rate of alleged staff sexual *misconduct* is 8.53 per 1,000 youth. With 103 total allegations (Beck & Hughes, 2005), the rate of alleged staff sexual *harassment* is 1.64 per 1,000. Thus, combining misconduct and harassment (640), the rate of alleged staff-on-youth sexual offenses is 10.17 per 1,000 youth.

However, another problem with using these data to estimate sexual violence is that several of the allegations could be untrue, or if true, difficult to substantiate. Most of the incidents reported in the 2004 BJS study were not substantiated. Authorities external to those working in correctional systems and facilities are often called on to conduct fair, objective investigations. However, external authorities such as police and child protective services were not always in charge of investigating allegations against staff. Among the 50 state juvenile systems, 18 reported that allegations of staff sexual misconduct were investigated by external authorities only, 18 reported that they shared investigations with external authorities, and 14 reported that investigations were conducted internally (Beck & Hughes, 2005). Among the 270 private and local juvenile facilities sampled, 156 reported that allegations of staff sexual misconduct were investigated by external authorities only, 45 reported that they shared investigations with external authorities, and 69 reported that investigations were conducted internally (Beck & Hughes, 2005).

In the 2004 study, authorities substantiated only 15.4% (69) of the investigated alleged incidents of staff sexual *misconduct* in state juvenile facilities (20 incidents were still being investigated). About 45% (204) were unsubstantiated and 39.1% (175) were unfounded (Beck & Hughes, 2005). In private/local juvenile facilities, 17.2% (11) of these incidents were substantiated (six were still being investigated), 53.1% (34) were unsubstantiated, and 29.7% (19) were unfounded. Regarding allegations of staff sexual *harassment*, authorities substantiated 30.8% (16) of the investigated incidents in state juvenile facilities (three were still being investigated), 51.9% (27) were unsubstantiated, and 17.3% (9) were unfounded. In private/local juvenile facilities, 13.0% (6) of these incidents were substantiated (two were still being investigated), 37.0% (17) were unsubstantiated, and 50.0% (23) were unfounded (Beck & Hughes, 2005). With a population of 62,935 and 80 total substantiated incidents in state and private/local facilities in 2004 (Beck & Hughes, 2005), the rate of substantiated staff sexual *misconduct* is 1.27 per 1,000 youth in custody. With 22 total substantiated incidents (Beck & Hughes, 2005), the rate of substantiated staff sexual *harassment* is 0.35 per 1,000. Thus, combining misconduct and harassment (102), the rate of substantiated staff-on-youth sexual offenses is 1.62 per 1,000 youth.

For 2005 and 2006, the BJS published a separate report on sexual violence in juvenile correctional facilities (Beck, Adams, & Guerino, 2008). This report combines the 2005 and 2006 surveys and is less descriptive. Again, all state juvenile systems (containing 501 facilities in 2004) were surveyed. In 2005, 205 private and 74 local facilities were sampled. In 2006, 272 private and 58 local facilities were sampled. Reported staff-on-youth sexual offenses decreased from the 2004 study. For 2005–06, the researchers estimated 1,314 staff sexual *misconduct* and 446 staff sexual *harassment* allegations nationally.

Misconduct and harassment were not separated in the reports of substantiated allegations. Authorities substantiated 13% (99) of the investigated allegations of staff sexual offenses in state juvenile systems (50 incidents were still being investigated), 29% (216) were unsubstantiated, and 58% (430) were unfounded (Beck et al., 2008). In private/local juvenile facilities, 22% (196) were substantiated (105 were still being investigated), 41% (357) were unsubstantiated, and 37% (321) were unfounded. The rate of substantiated incidents of staff-on-youth sexual offenses was 1.2 per 1,000 youth held (1.3 for state systems, 1.2 for local/private facilities) (Beck, Adams, & Guerino, 2008). This was noticeably down from the rate of 1.62 in 2004.

The BJS reports give good estimates of the number of *alleged* and *authority-substantiated* incidents of staff sexual offenses against juveniles in correctional facilities, but do not offer adequate estimates of the "real number" of these offenses. Like sexual offenses in the general population, those which take place in correctional facilities are likely under-reported. Beck and Hughes (2005) point out that victims may not report incidents to authorities because of personal embarrassment, fear of retaliation by the perpetrator, the inmate code of silence, and lack of trust in staff. Other problems with official data are that some allegations are hard to prove or untrue, and complete faith must be put in the ways that authorities investigate allegations and record, store, report, and share information. Thus, the BJS surveys of sexual violence reported by correctional authorities must be supplemented with other types of surveys. Victim surveys can be used to detect incidents that are undetected by official data collection.

Fortunately, the BJS's National Survey of Youth in Custody (NSYC) collects reports of sexual violence directly from juveniles in state facilities. Computer-assisted self-administered questionnaires were anonymously completed by 9,198 juveniles placed in 166 state-owned or operated and 29 locally or privately operated juvenile correctional facilities between June 2008 and April 2009. This sample represents 26,551 adjudicated youth held nationwide (Beck, Harrison, & Guerino, 2010). Staff sexual misconduct was distinguished by type and if force was used. Misconduct "excluding touching" included sexual intercourse, oral sex, or hand contact with genitals. "Other sexual contacts only" included acts such as kissing, looking at private body parts, and exposure to pornographic images. Force included actual or threatened physical force, pressuring, or coercion such as offering money or favors. The researchers applied sample weights to estimate national rates. Accordingly, about 10.3% (2,730) of youth reported one or more incidents of sexual victimization by facility staff in the past twelve months (or since admission). Staff-on-youth sexual misconduct rates in state facilities (10.9%) were higher than in private facilities (7.9%). About 4.3% (1,550) of youth reported forced or coerced sexual contact with staff; most of them (3.9% of youth) reported misconduct excluding touching. About 6.4% (1,710) reported non-forced or coerced sexual contact with staff; again, most of them (5.9% of youth) reported misconduct excluding touching. Of those reporting victimization by staff, about 88% reported being victimized more than once and 27% reported begin victimized more than ten times (Beck, Harrison, & Guerino, 2010).

A second NSYC was conducted between February and September 2012 (Beck et al., 2013). The second sample consisted of 8,707 youth in 273 state and 53 local or private facilities, representing 18,138 adjudicated youth held nationwide. This time the researchers estimated that only 7.7% (1,390) of youth reported sexual victimization by staff. Staff-on-youth sexual misconduct rates in state facilities (8.2%) were again higher than in private facilities (4.5%), though both declined from 2008–09. About 3.5% of youth reported forced or coerced sexual contact with staff; most of them (3.1% of youth) reported misconduct excluding touching. About 4.7% reported non-forced or coerced sexual contact with staff; most of them (4.3% of youth) reported misconduct excluding touching. Again, most youth reporting victimization by staff reported more than one incident (85.9%); 20.4% reported 11 or more incidents. Additional measures were added to the NSYC-2, and the researchers linked some of them to victimization rates. The decline in sexual victimization rates could be attributed to "fewer youth held in large facilities, a drop in average exposure time, and rising positive views of facility staff and fairness" (Beck et al., 2013, p. 10). Also, staff-on-youth sexual misconduct was linked to other inappropriate behaviors. For example, several youth reporting victimization by staff also reported that staff told them about their personal lives (69.1%), gave them special gifts (28.1%), or treated them as special or a favorite (63.6%) (Beck et al., 2013).

Also, the Office of Juvenile Justice and Delinquency Prevention (OJJDP) conducted its Survey of Youth in Residential Placement

(SYRP), which examined more than just sexual victimization. Youth were asked if they had, during their stay in their current facility, experienced theft ("personal property stolen when you weren't around to protect it"), robbery ("personal property taken by force or by threat"), physical assault or threat ("beaten up or threatened with being beaten up"), and sexual assault ("anyone forced you to engage in sexual activity") (Sedlack, McPherson, & Basena, 2013, p. 2). Computer-assisted self-administered questionnaires were anonymously completed by a nationally representative sample of 7,073 youth in 205 facilities during spring 2013. Forty-six percent (about 3,254) of youth reported theft. Of them, 19% (about 618) accused staff. Thus, about 8.7% of all youth reported that staff stole from them. Ten percent (about 707) of youth reported robbery. Of them, 41% (about 290) accused staff. Thus, about 4.1% of all youth reported that staff took their property by force or threat. Twenty-nine percent (about 2,051) of youth reported threatened or actual physical assault. Of them, 24% (about 492) accused staff. Thus, about 7% of all youth reported that staff threatened or beat them. Four percent (about 283) of youth reported sexual assault. Of them, 50% (about 142) accused staff. Thus, about 2% of all youth reported that staff sexually assaulted them (Sedlack, McPherson, & Basena, 2013). This sexual victimization rate is considerable lower than the ones from the NSYC studies, which may be due to different estimation procedures and the SYRP's use of a measure seemingly limited to forced physical sexual contact. Also, it should be acknowledged that some of the youth could have been accusing staff of theft or robbery on occasions when items were taken from them legitimately (contraband, restricted use, etc.).

As would be expected, the anonymous self-report surveys detected more victimization than official records (accounting for the fact that survey data analyses yielded mostly prevalence rates and official data analyses yielded incidence rates). For a variety of reasons, victims are often less willing to disclose to authorities. At the same time, it is possible that some survey participants do not provide accurate information. This inaccuracy, however, may involve both over-reporting—participants making up incidents or misinterpreting situations—and under-reporting—victims sometimes denying their own victimization (especially sexual) or being unwilling to divulge it even anonymously. It would be naïve to accept that employee-on-youth misconduct rates are as low as substantiation rates or as high as self-report rates. Perhaps the truth is "somewhere in the middle." Regardless, the rates estimated in the two survey studies may also seem low. However, these rates still suggest that the physical, sexual, and property victimization of youth by staff is occurring at unacceptable levels. It should also be kept in mind that many youths are victimized multiple times (as indicated in the BJS survey reports) and these studies detected only a few types of misconduct. It may be good news that the rates decreased over time in the BJS studies (including the survey). Changes in reporting, not the actual occurrence, of incidents may be a possible explanation, but it is plausible that PREA, decreased use of incarceration, and other changes are reducing the actual victimization of system-involved youth.

3.3 A GLOBAL PROBLEM

Like many, the problem of professional misconduct against youth is a global one. Not only does it occur worldwide but institutional maltreatment of youth is a violation of well-established, widely accepted international human rights standards and principles (Acoca, 1998). Most of the scholarship covered in this book stems from the United Kingdom, United States, and Canada. However, the Western literature does contain a few studies conducted in other countries.

Davidson-Arad (2005) studied staff and resident perceptions of violence and risky behavior by residents as well as staff abuse in three types of juvenile correctional facilities in Israel: diagnostic, closed, and (more community-based) hostels. Further, the study included both boys' and girls' facilities. Respondents indicated frequency of behaviors on a 1−5 scale (1 = never, 5 = very often) for multiple items measuring each type of behavior. Staff abuse of residents was measured with five items: cursing at/humiliating, slapping/pinching/pushing, sexually harassing, picking on, and intentionally destroying property. The mean responses to these items indicate relatively low perceived occurrence of these behaviors, with residents reporting significantly but not astonishingly more (staff = 1.16, residents = 1.67). Staff and residents reported more peer violence and risk behaviors (means ranging from 1.68 to 2.24) with staff indicating a bit more. More violence, risk behaviors, and staff abuse were reported by staff and residents in closed institutions. The researcher speculated that increased staff abuse in closed institutions could occur because their residents include serious offenders whom staff find more difficult to control and less protected by public sympathy and scrutiny. Significantly more risk behaviors, but not peer violence, was reported by staff and residents in boys' facilities. Noticeably more staff abuse was reported by staff and residents in girls' facilities, but the difference was not statistically significant. The researcher warns that respondent awareness, definitions of behaviors, and reporting tendencies likely play a part in these differences. Davidson-Arad (2005) reasoned that since the only acceptable level is "never," the small frequency of unsafe behavior including staff abuse in facilities constitutes a highly problematic "occasional occurrence."

Davidson-Arad and Golan (2007) later conducted Chi-square analyses of the Israeli juvenile corrections study that was restricted to youth-reported data. This analysis also separated type of victimization. Here, the researchers found significant gender differences. Regarding victimization by peers, juveniles in male facilities experienced higher rates of physical violence (boys = 26%, girls = 7.6%) and armed threats (boys = 18.8%, girls = 1.9%) while those in girls' facilities experienced higher rates of theft (girls = 64.8%, boys = 36.5%). Regarding victimization by staff, 32.3% of boys (32) and 20% of girls (21) reported physical abuse; 12.5% of boys (12) and 4.8% of girls (5) reported sexual abuse; 10.4% of boys (10) and 7.6% of girls (8) reported sexual harassment; and 32.3% of boys (32) and 31.4% of girls (33) reported verbal abuse. Only the differences in physical and sexual abuse were significant. In all, juveniles in boys' facilities had higher rates of the more severe forms of self-reported victimization including sexual abuse by staff (Davidson-Arad & Golan, 2007).

In another study in Israel, Attar-Schwartz (2011) examined verbal and physical maltreatment by staff in residential facilities. Anonymous self-report questionnaires were completed by 1,324 Jewish and Arab adolescents residing in 32 "at-risk youth" care settings (traditional group institutions, clusters of family homes, and combined residential group/family-like settings). Physical maltreatment was defined as being grabbed and shoved, pinched, slapped, kicked, or punched within the past month, and verbal maltreatment was defined as being cursed at, humiliated, insulted, or ridiculed within the past month. About 29% of youth reported being verbally maltreated at least once. Specifically, 15% reported cursing and 29.9% reported humiliation, insult, or ridicule. About 25% of youth reported being physically maltreated at least once. Specifically, 19.2% reported grabbing or shoving, 15.7% reported pinching, 11.7% reported slapping, and 11.1% reported kicking or punching. Attar-Schwartz (2011) describes these self-report rates as worrisome.

Kiessl and Würger (2002) examined victimization of incarcerated boys in South Africa as part of a survey conducted in 1998. South Africa has developed a modern juvenile justice system with the intention of abiding by United Nations standards for the treatment of juvenile offenders, including the prohibition of corporal punishment. In practice, however, South African juveniles may be treated as harshly as adult prisoners. Self-administered questionnaires were completed by 804 youth (under the age of 21) and 404 managerial and frontline correctional staff from 12 juvenile prisons and four "places of safety." (The youth sample contained only 21 girls, from one prison, who were excluded from this particular analysis.) Likely due to the controversial nature of questions, the study is restricted by a significant amount of missing data. Findings included the following. Roughly 45% of prison (N = 521) and place of safety (N = 230) youth respondents reported that they often observed staff-on-youth assault, while about 28% of prison and 15% of place of safety youth reported that they observed it rarely. Some youth reported that they had experienced illegal disciplinary measures (prevalence). Among 416 prison youth, 13.7% reported solitary confinement or isolation, 22.4% reported restriction of visits, 19.2% reported whipping, and 26.4% reported smacking. Among 148 place of safety youth, 4.7% reported solitary confinement or isolation, 18.2% reported restriction of visits, 19.6% reported whipping, and 33.8% reported smacking (Kiessl & Würger, 2002).

Kiessl and Würger (2002) also found evidence of failure to prevent youth-on-youth victimization. Of all reporting youth (N = 697), 20.5% reported experiencing assault, 3.7% reported experiencing sexual assault, and 6% reported experiencing both. Further, of 752 youth (most of the male sample), 66.7% reported observing assaults of others and 38.7% reported observing sexual assaults of others. Some staff confirmed the high occurrence of youth-on-youth violence: 80.4% of prison (N = 234) and 73.5% of place of safety staff reported that such offenses took place. Also, almost half (47.8%) of staff respondents (N = 364) reported that children under the age of 18 were not separated from older residents. Of youth who reported their peer victimization to staff (79 assault, 39 sexual assault), less than one third reported receiving a response from staff—of them about one third reported the reaction as negative (Kiessl & Würger, 2002). Comparable to studies conducted in North America and the United Kingdom, Kiessl and Würger's study suggests that a minority of youth are seriously victimized by staff, but that this victimization is prevalent enough to constitute a major problem.

3.4 CONCLUSION

The existing body of research is inadequate for determining good international, national, or even regional or state estimates of the extent of professional misconduct against youth in custody. The few large-scale studies were conducted on only a few of the more serious types of misconduct, and therefore provide but a partial picture of the overall problem. Other studies are not generalizable because they were confined to certain facilities or locales. Small studies do, however, show the potential for misconduct that can exist at a facility or agency. While much more research needs to be done, enough has been conducted to strongly suggest that professional misconduct against youth is relatively small in terms of its occurrence, but is a major problem in terms of its impact. A conclusion that globally, professional misconduct against youth in correctional treatment environments is likely at a level of frequency and seriousness above what is acceptable seems justified.

CHAPTER 4

Factors Contributing to Misconduct

Very few studies have empirically tested factors of professional misconduct against youth, and the few conducted tested a limited number of factors. Most literature sources stating the factors of misconduct are based on anecdotal evidence: professional experience, professional opinion, and reports of cases. While it may be apparent how some proposed factors work—improper screening that fails to prevent the hiring of known offenders, for example—it is still important to more thoroughly assess their impacts through objective research. Predatory tendencies of certain individuals and failure of screening to detect them explain serious violent and sexual forms of misconduct, but these are not representative of most forms. Thus, it is doubtful that these factors explain a great deal of the employee misconduct that takes place in youth work. Also, the impacts of some factors—organizational, community, and societal-level factors for example—may not be clear. Regardless, literature based on practical knowledge has identified plausible factors of employee misconduct.

4.1 INDIVIDUAL

Clearly, individual-level offender characteristics are major factors in explaining the occurrence of employee misconduct. Personality, moral character, and intelligence, for instance have much to do with the likelihood that misconduct will occur. Attitudes toward youth may also influence how employees treat them. For example, those with punitive attitudes may be more likely to use coercive power to achieve control over youth (Peterson-Badali & Koegl, 2002). Thus, hiring employees without the proper character, skill, and education requirements increases the likelihood of misconduct (Kay et al., 2007). According to Roush (2008), the inability to screen out adults who want to work with troubled youth for the wrong reasons plays an important role in the occurrence of sexual violence toward youth. Inadequate and lax recruitment, background investigation (i.e.

criminal history and references), and screening practices make it more likely that employees with abusive tendencies and/or the inability to properly care for youth under stressful circumstances will be hired. Relying on basic procedures such as criminal background and reference checks will insufficiently screen out employees highly capable of misconduct (Kay et al., 2007). Also, the panel interview is inadequate in terms of validity and reliability in screening out undesirable candidates (Skinner, 2003).

The inability to negotiate role conflicts and maintain appropriate professional relationship boundaries may also lead to distinct acts of misconduct (Davidson, 2004; Roush, 2008). Many acts of misconduct may be the result of poor judgment and improper role negotiation rather than ill intent. Employees often do not anticipate or intend their acts of misconduct. If they do not reflect on who they are and what their approach is to everyday work, they may find themselves engaging in misconduct—when they become too close to, or distant from, a child for example. Employees may not be enough aware of factors in their lives that influence their boundaries with youth at work—such as their socioeconomic status, upbringing, and own emotional needs—as well as situations at work that put them at increased risk of violating relationship boundaries (Davidson, 2004). Because they do not make conscious efforts to maintain proper boundaries with youth, some employees fail to prevent themselves from "slipping" into relationships that increase the likelihood of committing misconduct.

A fundamental problem that youth workers must overcome, then, is that of dual relationships (Roush, 2008). On one hand, youth workers are supposed to maintain a certain amount of professional distance from youth. This has several practical benefits for both employees and youth. On the other hand, youth workers are expected to nurture youth, which requires more of a social relationship. In many cases, staff may be the closest that a child has to "a family." Youth workers who view their work as a calling to help children are generally looked upon favorably. Indeed, much therapeutic value can be gained from a close relationship with a positive adult role model. Thus, the professional role of the youth worker is accompanied by a largely competing social role. Balancing these roles is very difficult, especially considering that policies regulating professional and social relationships tend to be inconsistent (Roush, 2008). Employees who fail to balance these roles are more likely to maltreat youth in their care. Davidson (2004) conceptualizes a continuum of professional relationship boundaries with the polar extremes constituting "entangled" and "rigid" in terms of the emotional connections and involvement workers have with youth and possibly their families. Both extremes stand as violations of the role of the professional child care worker. The worker who is authentic and caring toward the child while maintaining professional boundaries demonstrates balance, represented by the center of the continuum. Agencies that leave this role negotiation up to individual employee experience and discretion, without much support and direction from policy and training, will increase the likelihood that their employees will engage in misconduct.

Gender is a major factor in committing professional misconduct against youth. Similar to earlier research (e.g. Rosenthal et al., 1991), Blatt (1992) found that male staff members were more likely to be involved. Though men likely made up about half or less of residential care workers in the state, 75% of those accused of misconduct were men. Important, then, is the role that male aggression plays in the maltreatment of residential youth. Pringle (1993) argued that gender is a major factor in child sexual abuse committed by child care workers; in particular, masculinity increases men's potential to commit sexual abuse. However, misconduct by female professionals does occur, so it should not be overlooked. Also, research does not always implicate men as the main perpetrators. The US Bureau of Justice Statistics national self-report surveys covered earlier (Beck et al., 2013; Beck, Harrison, & Guerino, 2010) found that women were much more likely to be accused of sexually maltreating youth. Roughly 90–95% of self-reported victims (the victim group and general sample were predominately male) accused female staff which dipped only to roughly 80–85% when restricted to forced/coerced activity. This occurred despite the fact that women may have made up only about half of the represented workforce (about 42–44% of state facility staff). More research is needed to discover if certain circumstances increase women's likelihood to commit certain types of abuse. Also, comparing abuse between male youth workers and the general adult male population would help answer some important questions. Are male youth workers more, less, or equally likely to abuse children? Is the higher likelihood of male youth workers to abuse (compared to females) simply a reflection of men's higher likelihood to violently and sexually offend in general?

4.2 ORGANIZATIONAL AND INSTITUTIONAL

As mentioned earlier, faulty hiring practices increase the likelihood that individuals with undesirable characteristics will be hired. However, faulty hiring practices are not necessarily due to poor decision-making by individual administrators. Bureaucratic flaws reduce an organization's ability to prevent misconduct. Sometimes individuals predisposed to offend "slip through the cracks" in employee screening (Bloom, 1993). High turnover and pressure to hire leads to hiring shortcuts, and investigating agencies might be backlogged and not able to register an offender before one is hired. Also, offenders may simply be fired from past positions without formal charges made against them, and others may be skilled at deceit and thus able to avoid detection (Bloom, 1993). Though they well understand the costs of misconduct and the need to hire the right staff, managers may fail to make significant improvements to hiring processes because they are distracted by other pressing operational concerns or continue to be confident in their discretion in staff selection (Skinner, 2003).

Some former employees who have committed misconduct may go undetected because of the circumstances under which they exited prior employment. A failure to obtain a criminal conviction could interfere with justifying dismissal in a case of misconduct. Rather than pursuing the case to the full extent of the law, then, some administrators may simply accept a voluntary resignation from an employee who wants to avoid prosecution and punishment (Roush, 2008). While this has practical advantages for the agency at hand, the practice allows offenders to return to youth work at other agencies. According to Roush (2008), factors that hamper administrators' ability to fire dangerous staff include: delays in resolving disciplinary actions; prosecution methods less likely to produce criminal convictions; policies that require "beyond a reasonable doubt" instead of "a preponderance of the evidence" as the burden of proof for termination; and collective bargaining agreements that do not recognize some offenses as serious enough to warrant termination.

Even employees assessed to be low-risk can engage in misconduct if placed within an abusive employee culture (Kay et al., 2007). Organizational or institutional culture can promote residential victimization. For example, if an institution itself gives home to a "machismo culture" (perhaps similar to that of delinquent youth), staff will be less likely to intervene in bullying. Staff may believe that the victims are "wimps" and need to "toughen up" and that their bullies are just "joking around." Browne and Falshaw (1996, p. 126) state: "Threats of violence, bullying and intimidation are more likely to occur when the institution fails to take the issue seriously and where staff use intimidation to manage and control young people." Insular and closed-staff cultures in organizations can interfere with the reporting of staff misconduct.

Staff members may not report misconduct on the part of other employees because of fear of reprisal and reliance on the accused to get along well at work, as in handling violent outbreaks by residents (Asbridge, 2007). Permissive or rebellious informal staff structures combined with vague or ill-defined policies and procedures lead to a culture that promotes staff misconduct and hinders its prevention, identification, and intervention. While policies typically prohibit clear acts of misconduct, many may fail to properly regulate other behaviors that contribute to the workplace culture. For example, some agencies may not have clear written rules regulating the ways that employees dress, speak, and respect youths' privacy. Inappropriate dress (e.g. revealing clothes and violent T-shirts), profanity, and invading youths' personal space contribute to sexualized, violent, and/or other hostile environments that promote misconduct (Roush, 2008). Also, these behaviors will often constitute misconduct in and of themselves.

In addition to the conflicting demands placed upon them, youth workers are often overworked and underpaid, have little say in decision-making, and receive little support in general. Job stressors may include taxing staff-to-child ratios and overcrowding, threats of lay-offs, and movements of children to different living areas (Kendrick, 1998). In a study of 45 residential workers and managers from a local authority service in the United Kingdom, Horwath (2000) found that 87% (39) of respondents cited insufficient staff on duty to manage a situation as a justification for poor practices described in vignettes. In a study of reports of alleged maltreatment by residential workers in New York State, Blatt (1992) found younger workers were more likely to be involved. Workers younger than 35 were overrepresented as alleged perpetrators while those 35 and older were underrepresented. Twenty-five to thirty-four-year-olds made up about 46% of alleged perpetrators but only about 30% of total workers. Those younger than 25 years of age made up about 20% of alleged perpetrators but only about 6% of all workers. About 66% of the reports involved those between 20 and 29. Similar to young parents, young youth workers may experience further stress due to the pressures of establishing a career, financial difficulties, and learning new roles (Blatt, 1992). Thus, youth workers are highly susceptible to burnout and job dissatisfaction, which makes them more likely to maltreat children. Over time, a stressed youth worker may develop increasingly negative attitudes toward youth in care and a pattern of reacting impulsively and impatiently toward them. This may include a tendency to seek physical solutions in dealing with oppositional youth (Kendrick, 1998).

Improper training on how to interact with and supervise youth increases misconduct. Roush (2008) complains of a lack of staff training in maintaining professional boundaries with youth. Staff-youth boundaries are an important part of the organizational structure and functioning of the agency. They constitute limits on what kinds of interactions are allowed in staff—youth relationships and protect youth with various needs and vulnerabilities. Unambiguous expectations regarding professional staff conduct illuminate the separation of youth and employee roles. Without clear, understandable, and equitably enforced rules of employee—youth relationships, these boundaries may not be honored, which puts the emotional and physical safety of both employee and youth in jeopardy. Insufficient training makes staff less able to recognize relationship limits and therefore refrain from committing boundary violations with youth (Roush, 2008). Also, employees often lack the training needed to properly care for children with special needs. In addition to histories of abuse and neglect, many children enter placements with severe emotional, behavioral, and developmental problems, as well as other disabilities that make them difficult to manage and treat (Hobbs, Hobbs, &Wynne, 1999). Without enough compassion, education, and skill, employees may intentionally or unintentionally respond to disordered children's behavior in abusive ways.

Problems with organizational structure facilitate misconduct. Disorganization inhibits responsibility for preventing and detecting maltreatment of youth, accountability for incidents of maltreatment, and complaint systems available to youth and employees (Kendrick, 1998). This includes understaffing. Violence is more likely to occur where there is not enough staff to supervise (Roush, 2008). Also, a lack of managerial personnel and direct manager contact with units makes it less likely that management will prevent or detect maltreatment (Kendrick, 1998). Further, maltreatment is facilitated by coercive, pessimistic administrative styles. These are characterized by autocratic leadership that discourages staff and resident participation in decision-making; an emphasis on handling difficult children and control; a belief in distant and dehumanized relationships with youth; and an oppressor mentality that promotes hostility toward females, children, or minorities (Siskind, 1986, cited in Kendrick, 1998).

Similar to earlier research (e.g. Rosenthal et al., 1991), Blatt (1992) found that alleged incidents of maltreatment by residential staff are more likely to occur between 5:00 and 11:00 pm and between 7:00 and 8:00 am. These are potentially the most chaotic times in a residential facility. Then, youth are more likely to be in the unit, awake, and active (e.g. getting up and ready in the morning and finishing dinner and preparing for bed in the evening), but administrators and practitioners are less likely to be working and there are fewer program activities. These conditions place staff members under a great deal of stress which, again, may increase their likelihood of maltreating youth. Further, the absence of extensively trained professionals means that appropriate responses to incidents (e.g. medical care, psychological care, removing the child or worker from the facility, and timely reporting) may not occur (Blatt, 1992).

Maltreatment of children by employees is more likely to occur if managers deny that it can occur in their programs (Kendrick, 1998). Some may believe that "it doesn't happen here." With such a false sense of security, administrators and staff may not be vigilant enough to prevent or detect child maltreatment. This denial may be promoted by institutions' reluctance to report incidents of maltreatment due to fears of damaged reputation, financial losses, legal problems, and lack of placement alternatives for the maltreated child (Kendrick, 1998). The more open institutions are about incidents of maltreatment, the more others may realize that maltreatment is a system- and profession-wide threat that affects all facilities and programs.

The nature of residential placement itself puts children at increased risk of professional maltreatment (Kendrick, 1998). Facilities are physically, geographically, and socially isolated from the outer community. They are "closed systems" that determine their own policies and procedures and restrict contact with families, other professionals, and the public. The wider community then tends to be unaware of what goes on in these institutions. Further, placed children have very little power; they have little voice in decisions concerning their protection and care, and isolation means that they have few outlets for expressing their concerns. Some children also have developmental lags, disabilities, and other characteristics that further decrease their ability to look after their own interests (Kendrick, 1998). Thus, misconduct against youth is more likely to occur in programs that do not facilitate external oversight and children's contact with the outer community; isolated, powerless children are more likely to be victimized.

During the 1980s and 1990s, the Unites States experienced both a tremendous growth in the number of incarcerated juveniles and a decrease in the resources needed to 1) supply facilities with the capacity to meet the basic human needs of youth and 2) externally monitor the conditions under which these youth live. Acoca (1998) explains that this lack of sustenance and oversight has a particularly egregious effect on girls. Because girls make up such a small portion of offenders, they may be relatively "invisible" in a system largely tailored to the needs of males. The specific emotional and physical needs of girls in placements—e.g. clean, appropriate clothing, reproductive health care, and outdoor recreation and exercise—therefore may be neglected. Failure to adequately meet the needs of pregnant girls, in particular, harms not only their health but the health of their children (Acoca, 1998).

4.3 VICTIM CHARACTERISTICS

Though not *causes of maltreatment*, characteristics of children in placement can serve as vulnerability factors placing them at higher risk of being victimized by professionals. Gender is one such factor. Blatt (1992) examined a random sample of 510 reports of residential child abuse and neglect allegations made to the New York State Child Abuse and Maltreatment Register. The cases involved facilities licensed or operated by the Department of Social Services (49%), Office of Mental Health (25%), Office of Mental Retardation and Developmental Disabilities (8%), and Division for Youth (18%). Males were somewhat more likely to be the alleged victim in the reports. (Risk according to age was not detected: the age distribution of alleged victims did not significantly differ from that of all residential youth.) Boys were involved in 75% of alleged incidents but made up 67% of children in the state's residential care (Blatt, 1992). However, it should be noted here that this comparison does not break down types of mal-treatment—sexual vs. non-sexual physical, for example. Earlier research suggested that institutionalized girls are at higher risk of sexual abuse and that boys are at higher risk of physical abuse (Groze, 1990; Rosenthal et al., 1991). However, as mentioned earlier, Davidson-Arad and Golan (2007) found in an Israeli sample of incar-cerated juveniles that boys reported a significantly higher rate of sexual abuse than girls and that boys and girls did not significantly differ in sexual harassment.

Attar-Schwartz's (2011) study of Israeli residential youth included multivariate analyses of individual- and facility-level correlates of physical and verbal maltreatment by staff. Gender was the strongest individual-level predictor of physical abuse, with boys at higher risk, though gender did not predict verbal abuse (age was insignificant). Boys may experience more abuse by staff because they tend to be more aggressive, drawing staff into more confrontations, and like many people, staff may see physical responses as more appropriate for boys. Emotional symptoms, hyperactivity, and perceived strictness were positively related to both physical and verbal abuse. Perceived caretaker support and favorable views of anti-violence policy were neg-atively related to both physical and verbal abuse. Also, "rehabilitative" facilities serving lower-risk youth were associated with less physical abuse compared to "therapeutic" facilities serving higher-risk youth. These results are consistent with the notion that youth workers are more likely to maltreat youth who are more difficult to understand and manage. Attar-Schwartz (2011) cautions that since the data were cross-sectional, causal direction cannot be established. In some cases the state of a variable would have existed before the abuse (gender for example), but it is possible that residents' perceptions were developed after the abuse.

Past research has given very little attention to the impact of race and ethnicity. One exception is that Attar-Schwartz (2011) found that Arab youth in residential facilities were more likely to report physical and verbal abuse by staff than Jewish youth. The few existing inqui-ries into race and ethnicity tend to be descriptive and contradictory.

For example, the US Bureau of Justice Statistics' national self-report surveys covered earlier (Beck et al., 2013; Beck, Harrison, & Guerino, 2010) found that black youth reported slightly higher rates of sexual victimization by staff than white and Hispanic youth. Groze (1990), however, found that white juveniles were over-represented in allegations of mistreatment by staff in records from one southwestern state in the US. Thus, more research in this area is needed. Considering evidence of differential treatment of minorities in other areas of juvenile corrections, it could be hypothesized that racial and ethnic minorities are at increased risk of maltreatment by youth service professionals.

Individual Level Offender Characteristics

    Predatory Tendencies

    Lack of Education and Skill

    Coercive, Over-Punitive Attitudes and Beliefs toward Youth

    Inability to Negotiate Conflicting Roles

    Inability to Maintain Proper Relationship Boundaries with Youth

    Gender/Masculinity

Organizational and Institutional Level Factors

    Faulty Employment Practices (Screening, Hiring, and Firing)

    Unclear Policies and Procedures Guiding Employee–Youth Interactions

    Ill-Structured Formal Organizational Cultures

    Hostile Informal Organizational Cultures

    Stressful Work Conditions

    Inadequate Training

    Inadequate Staffing

    Coercive, Autocratic, and Distant Managerial Styles

    Denial of Presence of Threat, Lack of Vigilance

    Environmental Isolation

    Children's Lack of Social Power

    Lack of Public Resources Dedicated to Youth Work

Victim Characteristics

    Gender

    Disabilities/Disorders

    Race/Ethnicity?

Figure 4.1 Factors contributing to professional misconduct against youth.

4.4 CONCLUSION

Much more research is needed to properly identify the factors that cause or facilitate professional misconduct against youth. Still, the literature identifies several plausible factors that researchers and field professionals should be concerned with. Both individual offender and organizational- and institutional-level characteristics cause or facilitate misconduct, and some characteristics make youth more vulnerable to victimization. To summarize, more specific variables are listed in Figure 4.1. To properly understand causation behind professional misconduct against youth, models must extend beyond individual-level variables and account for factors operating at multiple social levels. This includes, but is not limited to, organizational- and institutional-level characteristics. Focusing on a few factors creates a misunderstanding of misconduct that inhibits efforts to solve the problem.

CHAPTER 5

Solutions to the Problem of Misconduct

Child protection is inextricably tied to the rationale for the very existence of juvenile service agencies, including those which securely detain youth. Thus, they are responsible for taking diligent action to prevent professional misconduct against youth and properly responding to it when it unfortunately does occur. A reactive approach to misconduct—simply punishing or firing employees who commit misconduct, for example—is very insufficient. Undoubtedly, several agencies do a fine job preventing, detecting, investigating, and resolving cases of misconduct against youth. However, even these agencies should continuously search for improvements to be made to anti-misconduct policies and practices. For instance, Pihl-Buckley (2008) points out that an agency's current rules against sexual misconduct can be adjusted in accordance with the Prison Rape Elimination Act (PREA) of 2003. Following the enactment of PREA, the Massachusetts Department of Youth Services (DYS) engaged in self-examination and determined that although it was doing well with its current policies and practices, there was room for improvement. Pihl-Buckley (2008, p. 47) writes:

> The Massachusetts DYS believes that it is responsible for asking three basic questions: Are the agency's policies and practices fair? Are they consistent? And, do they make sense? This self-assessment will keep both staff and youths safe by ensuring that the youths in DYS care are treated with respect and dignity.

Asbridge (2007) urges administrators to become familiar with and use current resources available to them, such as those offered by the National Institute of Corrections (NIC). With technical assistance from the NIC and a consulting group, the Massachusetts DYS became a leader in implementing PREA's mandate of safety in both juvenile and adult correctional facilities (Pihl-Buckley, 2008). The DYS used its PREA implementation plan to improve existing policies, practices, and procedures regarding sexual misconduct. The agency formed an internal PREA workgroup at the commissioner's level that "included representatives from the legal unit, investigations, clinical and medical services, the training academy, victim services, and community and facility operations" and later other state agencies as subcommittee members (Pihl-Buckley, 2008, p. 44). Under agreement with the NIC and through appraisal by the consultant, Massachusetts DYS created PREA implementation policies that serve as models for other states (Pihl-Buckley, 2008).

Many threats to the safety of youth are connected to problems with institutional and organizational culture. Thus, agencies must create the kind of workplace culture that will reduce and expose abuse, neglect, and other cases of misconduct. In implementing PREA, the Massachusetts DYS developed policies and practices aimed at sending the clear message to employees and youth that sexual misconduct will not be tolerated. New policies focused on "raising staff awareness of the 'red flags' around sexual misconduct, institutional culture, the impact of staff's individual behavior on the institutional culture, and the importance of professionalism" (Pihl-Buckley, 2008, p. 44). The policies also promoted an atmosphere in which youth feel more comfortable and safe reporting misconduct to staff. Youth were to be educated about the behavior they should expect from staff, including being informed that "consensual" sexual relationships with staff or other youth in custody are inappropriate and that staff's responsibility is to keep them safe. To ensure that these messages reached all organizational levels, the policies were followed by training, first for all DYS managers in state and private provider programs, and then by all state and provider staff. Specific issues and questions regarding implementation of PREA and the new agency policies arose during this initial training that required clarification. Concerns included: professional culture within a facility; communication between shifts, departments, management and staff, and program units; an atmosphere encouraging youth to make progress in treatment; access to reports of sexual misconduct; and disallowing a sexualized work environment. Staff members serve as role models and are in charge of creating a positive environment for youth. Regarding a sexualized work environment, then, employees suggested that current policies regarding dress code and language be reviewed and monitored to maintain consistent application across programs and prevent mixed messages about misconduct. The training department then prepared a report of these concerns to be addressed with continued dialogue (Pihl-Buckley, 2008).

Solving the problem of professional misconduct against youth requires several strategies, which may be generally categorized as prevention, detection, and intervention. Detection and intervention not only ensure that victimized youth and other affected parties receive remedies, but they also reduce incidents by contributing to the prevention of further acts of misconduct.

5.1 PREVENTION

To a large extent, youth safety is increased through effective treatment programming in general. For example, providing numerous constructive activities keeps youths engaged in pro-social behavior, thereby reducing idle time and room confinement and subsequently avoiding opportunities for employee or youth misconduct (Pihl-Buckley, 2008). Improving basic living conditions also reduces youth-on-youth misconduct, and is a task required of youth workers at all levels. As Kiessl and Würger (2002, p. 323) assert, peer violence among placed youth "results from a lack of care, lack of activities, the strong presence of subcultural phenomena, missing role models, and the scarcity of life necessities." Youth safety is another goal that can be achieved through the use of research evidence-supported best and promising practices, including those tailored to the needs of girls (Acoca, 1998). Also, Hobbs, Hobbs, and Wynne (1999) point out that better protection is achieved through effective individualized treatment planning. Children become more vulnerable when plans are not created and implemented in ways that recognize and meet special needs, as well as provide proper supervision. However, because placed youth are at higher risk of victimization due to factors present before and during placement, their special needs should include extra protections from maltreatment (Hobbs, Hobbs, & Wynne, 1999). Several specific strategies are required to prevent employee-on-youth misconduct. To create a strong anti-misconduct organizational culture, agencies must strengthen both *formal* structures—policies, procedures, recruitment, and hiring—and *informal* staff structures through good and clear definitions of misconduct, training, and supervision (Roush, 2008).

5.1.1 Policies and Procedures
It is essential that administrators develop comprehensive anti-misconduct policies and procedures (Roush, 2008). Bloom (1993, p.104) points out that the prevention of staff-on-child sexual abuse "begins with a clear policy statement that the agency's mission is protecting and caring for children, and that any sexual activity between staff members

and clients of any age is forbidden and will lead to dismissal and criminal prosecution." Asbridge (2007, p. 84) identifies "a strong network of policies and procedures built around best practices" that establishes a clear code of ethics and employee conduct as a major part of a strategy for addressing sexual assault of youth in juvenile corrections. Also, feedback from children, including complaints, should be considered in reviews, planning, and decision-making (Kendrick, 1998).

Much can be gained by adhering to a well-established professional code of ethics, such as those established by the American Correctional Association (Roush, 2008) and the National Association of Social Workers (Davidson, 2004). Not only should management ensure that their staff abide by such codes, but all employees as individuals should take it upon themselves to learn and abide by such codes. Employees are often faced with ethical dilemmas and cannot always rely on a higher authority to resolve them, especially if a decision must be made in the moment. It is often difficult to determine "the right thing to do." While professional codes of ethics often cannot dictate exactly what to do (Davidson, 2004), they are the result of deliberation by experienced professionals over time and therefore constitute a useful guide for ethical decision-making in everyday practice.

Policies are needed to maintain professional relationship boundaries between employees and youth—to guide, even restrict (but not eliminate), employee discretion regarding interaction with youth. Roush (2008) argues on behalf of policies regulating staff dress, staff language, and resident privacy. Such policies not only forbid acts of misconduct but also help establish proper staff–youth boundaries and contribute to a culture of professionalism and safety. Staff dress codes would necessarily vary depending on particular environment. For example, secure correctional facilities may require uniforms while more informal clothing (e.g. blue jeans and khaki pants) may be appropriate in residential facilities intended to offer a more "homelike" environment. While dress codes should not be unnecessarily rigid, it is to the agency's benefit to limit employee discretion regarding clothing worn at work. Profanity, however, is a different matter. To contribute to a safer, therapeutic, professional environment non-conducive to misconduct, it is necessary to virtually prohibit profanity, identifying a list of specific words (occasionally there may be valid use of profanity, as in therapy or reporting). However, discretion should be used in disciplining employees who use profanity, as overly harsh punishment delivered to an otherwise good employee can work against the agency's interests. Although significant limits on privacy are necessary for security in most youth offender treatment environments, youths must be protected from invasions of privacy that are unnecessary or put them at risk of victimization. Privacy is essential to the safety of confined youth (Roush, 2008). Policies establishing privacy boundaries help define unacceptable employee behaviors and reduce opportunities for employee-on-youth misconduct.

Regarding workplaces with a union, collective bargaining agreements can also play a larger part in prohibiting employee misconduct. Roush (2008, p. 34) suggests a dialogue with staff during training that addresses the tension between employee rights and the protection of youth, with the result of "some type of agreement between labor and management on a set of designated behaviors relating to staff sexual misconduct that warrant specific disciplinary action independent of the progressive discipline system."

Documented policies themselves will not prevent employee misconduct; they must be applied through effective supervision. It is also essential that administrators monitor and observe facilities to ensure that anti-misconduct policies and procedures are implemented in everyday practice and operations (Roush, 2008). Administrators thus should be in the practice of assessing supervision of youth schemes used at facilities. These include reliance on secondary supervision (e. g., camera or security booth) over primary supervision, setting staff-to-youth ratios, training staff to properly supervise and manage youth, policy on private one-on-one staff–youth interactions, and recognizing blind areas that could be used to hide inappropriate behavior (Asbridge, 2007). To maintain safety in child care environments, it is also necessary that agencies themselves are supervised by external authorities. All children's services should be regularly inspected by oversight agencies and standardized inspection report formats should be widely used for easier monitoring (Kendrick, 1998). Freundlich, Avery, and Padgett (2007, p. 184) recommend "Regular, announced site visits by licensing or contracting authorities that include private interviews with youth outside the presence of staff" to ensure that agencies operating congregate care facilities comply with safety regulations.

5.1.2 Hiring

Based on their interviews with stakeholders and former residents, Freundlich, Avery, and Padgett (2007) concluded that much more attention needs to be given to staffing congregate care settings. Kay et al. (2007) identify the development of safer employee recruitment and selection procedures as an important strategy for protecting children in residential settings. Since high-risk employees are more easily hired through lax selection practices, one basic prevention strategy is to carry out all phases of hiring thoroughly and carefully. Hiring should be a standardized process, with room for wise discretion, that is well organized and utilizes helpful resources.

Hiring must begin with a well-advertised announcement that thoroughly describes the job and candidate qualification profile, followed by intensive screening, interviewing, and selection procedures (Kendrick, 1998). Freundlich, Avery, and Padgett (2007) recommend that congregate care agencies consider involving youth in staff selection processes. Screening should explicitly address applicants' attitudes toward the control and punishment of children, as well as issues of power and sexuality (Kendrick, 1998) and their potential for inducing peer-on-peer violence (Peterson-Badali & Koegl, 2002). Safer hiring procedures involve collecting all relevant information about a candidate's past and an assessment of one's capabilities. Assessment could include exercises (written, group, etc.), aptitude and personality tests, and group and individual interviews that potentially include children. Short-list candidates should be required to visit the program site and meet with staff and youth (Kendrick, 1998).

Reference and background checks must be taken very seriously. In addition to criminal records checks, managers should (legally and ethically) utilize other information systems that identify individuals with professional misconduct histories (Kendrick, 1998). Reference checks should gather information about a candidate's strengths, weaknesses, and disciplinary history and perhaps, with permission from the candidate, the referee's assessment of the candidate's potential for maltreating youth (Kendrick, 1998).

Skinner (2003) describes the development of a "toolkit" of methods and materials that can be adapted to hiring for a variety of positions in youth social work: "Safer Recruitment and Selection for Staff Working in Childcare," originally published by the Scottish Executive in 2001. The toolkit was created by a Scottish Recruitment and Selection Consortium made up of four local social work authorities. It was adapted from human resource management best practices to fit social work staff selection. After six months of thorough analysis, sets of competencies (capabilities) were developed for each of 18 roles, ranging from first line practitioner to regional or national manager, using a commercial competency profiling software package. Next, expert panels and local steering groups gave the competencies more user-friendly language and made them more setting-specific, and a national consultation process assessed the utility of the competencies across a wider range of organizations. The Consortium then devised the "Selection Centre," a model comprised of psychometric tests and group and individual exercises used for addressing the competencies. The tests assess verbal, numerical, and abstract reasoning abilities and profile personality, and the exercises allow candidates to demonstrate their qualifications for the job. Tests and exercises contain simulations of aspects of the job and candidate performance is observed and scored against role capabilities by trained selectors. Additionally, specially-trained selectors conduct personal interviews to judge if candidates' approaches to important issues such as sexuality and punishment are consistent with social work values and ethics. Scores combining data from all of these activities are then used to determine the most suitable candidate(s) for a position (Skinner, 2003).[1]

Many Selection Centres were tested and the Scottish Executive's toolkit was to be implemented in hiring processes for all staff working with children in out-of-home placements across Scotland. Skinner (2003) warned that the model needs continued improvements and is not the complete answer to the problem of employee misconduct (presumably, many improvements have been made to the toolkit since 2001). In fact, the model may someday be replaced with something better. Though the use of rigorous systematic procedures is valuable in that it reduces problems associated with subjectivity and bias, some decisions will still require sound professional judgment. Also, safer selection must be accompanied by safer management structures and processes (e.g. staff supervision, appraisal, development, and training and disciplinary, grievance, and complaints procedures) and external scrutiny. However, the toolkit is a carefully researched and road-tested

---

[1]Those interested in the toolkit should contact the Scottish Executive.

attempt to build upon traditional hiring methods and embodies "evidence-based practice, life-long learning and a philosophy of continuous improvement" (Skinner, 2003, p. 35).

It is important for hiring processes to account for cultural contexts. The Scottish Executive's toolkit can also be used as an international model. Skinner (2003) describes the application of the model to the selection process for managers for two new residences in New Zealand. The main task was to devise exercises and tests (Selection Centre) that account for the local cultural aspects of youth work. A process was developed that aimed to ensure that the manager would be one who understands and respects children's cultural backgrounds, especially of Māori (indigenous) youth, and to avoid disadvantaging candidates because of their backgrounds. This process included a Māori Knowledge Assessment in psychometric testing and consultation with a Māori cultural adviser in determining the Selection Centre short-listing (Skinner, 2003).

Safer recruitment and selection only responds to one of the many types of factors of misconduct: personal factors. One must be careful not to assume that misconduct problems are simply due to a few "bad apples" that can be weeded out with better hiring practices. Better hiring practices will have limited results if nothing is done to respond to the threat of an abusive employee culture, for example. Hiring practices are also limited by a context that makes it difficult to find and hire attractive employees. Youth work is often associated with relatively low pay, undesirable working conditions, low professional status, lack of advancement opportunities, and pessimism or ambivalence concerning the value of residential youth care (despite that it is often a positive choice for some children). Thus, the working conditions of staff must also be examined; competitive salaries and benefits, and support and skilled supervision on the job would attract and retain better staff (Freundlich, Avery, & Padgett, 2007). Regardless of the challenges of hiring good employees, as an important child protection strategy, safer recruiting and selection can be embedded in a child welfare-oriented employee culture (Kay et al., 2007).

5.1.3 Training
In addition to screening and incentives, sufficient staffing includes continuous training of employees after being hired. In fact, PREA calls

for training that sufficiently ensures that staff members understand and appreciate the significance of and need to eliminate sexual assault in correctional facilities (Roush, 2008). Training ensures that practice does not stagnate; it brings new ideas and practices into the program and encourages employees to reassess their current approaches and procedures (Kendrick, 1998). Training addresses issues such as employee—youth boundaries, proper child development and care, and supervision/protection.

Roush (2008) argues that staff must be provided with more pre-service education and training on staff—youth boundary violations. Both youth and staff are physically and emotionally safer when rules are clear, understandable, and equitably enforced and when their boundaries are honored. Thus, it is important that staff become highly capable of recognizing relationship limits and refrain from altering boundaries with youth (Roush, 2008). By maintaining proper boundaries, employees can prevent themselves from engaging in interactions that constitute misconduct or increase the likelihood of committing misconduct. To avoid boundary violations, however, one must be aware of and understand factors that influence boundaries—including one's own background, socialization, and emotional needs—as well as situations that put one at risk of violating boundaries (Davidson, 2004). The Massachusetts DYS PREA implementation plan requires PREA training for employees during pre-employment and annually thereafter (Pihl-Buckley, 2008). This three-hour training facilitates discussion on boundary issues faced by staff in the workplace, raises awareness about specific situations that they may encounter when working with youth, and makes them aware that "they should never do anything for or with youths that they would not want their co-workers to know about" (Pihl-Buckley, 2008, p. 45).

Even after training, maintaining proper boundaries is a solution that depends heavily on individual employee discretion. Policies and procedures guide this discretion, but the youth care worker must possess and utilize critical thinking skills to apply rules and decide how to act when the rules do not dictate exactly what to do. In one extreme, an employee makes a poor or immoral decision to act in a way that harms a child. In another extreme, the employee avoids all interactions with youth, which may put them at risk of being accused of misconduct, including neglect of those interactions that are needed for healthy child development. Child care workers tend to be very worried about situations with youth that could get them into trouble, making them approach youth work "with gloves on" (Horwath, 2000). To avoid neglect, workers must be provided with ways to manage their warranted concerns about the professional risks of caring for youth.

Davidson (2004) illustrates proper discretion and role negotiation with boundaries of touch—hugging specifically. Occasionally, a child may appear to benefit from or even request the comforting assurance of a hug. What should employees do in these cases? Refraining from hugging would protect the employee from damaging accusations of inappropriate touch and perhaps becoming too close with the child; however, it may also convey rejection and be insensitive to the child's emotional needs, which could be especially harmful to youth who have been emotionally maltreated and/or have experienced severe loss. Generally, hugging is an important way to meet a child's emotional needs. Usually, institutionalized youth are no different than non-institutionalized youth in this regard. However, while the ulterior motives of youth should not be overestimated, some will seek physical contact for inappropriate reasons. Some will have a mixture of proper and improper motives. Here, the employee interested in maintaining balanced boundaries would carefully assess contextual factors such as the child's history and behavior, physical location at the time, and type of program or facility (secure facilities for serious offenders, for example, may prohibit affectionate touch). Then, one can decide if hugging is appropriate or not. On the other hand, refusing hugs even when the context warrants it demonstrates rigid boundaries, while hugging when it does not—when a child reacts negatively to touch for example—demonstrates entangled boundaries (Davidson, 2004). Of course, lack of physical contact is only a problem when youth have a need for it; a child who does not want friendly touch should not be touched.

Ward (1999) offers professional insights on strategic touch with youth. Knowing when and when not to touch obviously involves knowledge of laws, organizational policies, and program practices. However, it also involves knowledge of the meaning and impact of different kinds of touch as they exist in processes of child development, as well as the skills and support to put this knowledge into practice. Skill and support here is provided through training, teamwork, and guidance and backing from leadership. Some kinds of touch are often harmless or even helpful, assuming they are properly intended by the youth worker and interpreted by the youth: "nurturing" (necessary for physical care of the child); "incidental" (by-product of another activity such as teaching or working on tasks with youth); "communication" (emotional expressions—tenderness, sympathy, encouragement, etc.); "play" (part of constructive fun activities); and "healing" (comforting, therapeutic contact). Forms of touching to be prohibited are "controlling" (aggressive touching, grabbing, or physical punishment) and of course "sexual" touch. Workers must understand that youth with histories of abuse may be more likely to interpret—sometimes misinterpret—a touch as controlling, sexual, or otherwise problematic, but that avoiding all physical contact with them is not the answer. They will still have the need for human contact and to learn the difference between appropriate and inappropriate touch. Ward (1999) recommends that practitioners and staff work closely and cooperatively as a team to collect information on each child's prior experiences with physical contact, observe them daily to identify patterns and needs, make subsequent decisions on how touch fits into their individualized treatment, and then use experiences with strategic touch (including non-touch) to inform further policy and practice. Ward (1999) also comments that workers (individually and as a team) must consider their own feelings about touch, find out youths' feelings about touch by directly asking and talking to them, reduce misunderstandings by including verbal communication with touch, and include youth in policy- and practice-relevant discussions about physical contact in the program. With knowledge and open communication, then, inappropriate touch, misinterpretations, and much of the anxiety over the use of touch can be avoided.

The stressful nature of youth work makes self-reflection more difficult to maintain. However, youth workers can maintain proper boundaries through ongoing consultation with others and by taking care of themselves (Davidson, 2004). In youth care settings, staff must work together in teams, which fosters a climate of interpersonal consultation about how to perform youth work. Boundaries with clients are less likely to be violated in settings where staff members communicate openly and honestly. It is important that staff share perspectives and ask questions about their work with youth. Davidson (2004, p. 39) writes "Speaking with co-workers and appropriate experts on an ongoing basis about the choices and dynamics within one's professional relationships establishes the critical elements of accountability and perspective." To be able to meet the emotional needs of youth and handle the variety of stressors confronted in youth work, employees must themselves be emotionally healthy. Personal issues such as isolation, depression, and lack of support, along with stressful life events, make one emotionally vulnerable. An emotionally vulnerable employee is more likely to violate boundaries with youth. Like anyone else, it is important that youth workers take action to maintain emotional health. However, since they are responsible for the care and development of children, and one must be emotionally healthy to carry out this responsibility, youth workers are also ethically responsible for maintaining their own emotional health. Davidson (2004) mentions several specific strategies for preventing compassion fatigue ("burnout"). These include having friends outside of work, maintaining an identity separate from the professional role, collecting and reading letters of thanks from clients and co-workers, getting rest, and refraining from indulging in harmful substances.

Some research shows that male child welfare professionals are more likely, compared to their female counterparts, to commit abuse. Thus, training may include asking men to reflect on the role of masculinity in committing abuse, including its possible connections to beliefs, attitudes, assumptions, feelings, and desires that underlie tendencies to maltreat youth. Instead of being avoidant or defensive about the issue, men should be willing to openly discuss it regardless of how uncomfortable revelations may be. Pringle (1993) even asserts that all men have more potential (compared to women) to abuse youth in their care, and that by confronting this potential they are more able to diffuse it.

Some maltreatment may be due to child socialization beliefs and habits that are inappropriate for working with youth with special needs, such as lay theories concerning the effectiveness of punishment in shaping desirable child behavior. Some staff members may also lack an understanding of child cognitive, emotional, and behavioral development. Accordingly, Freundlich, Avery, and Padgett (2007, p. 185) argue that congregate youth care staff must be provided with training on "adolescent development and behavior, behavior management, conflict resolution, maintaining control in group and residential care settings, and developing constructive relationships with youth." Since punitive and utilitarian attitudes may increase staff's tendencies to achieve control through peer-on-peer violence, Peterson-Badali and Koegl (2002) recommend that juvenile correctional staff be provided with pre-service and in-service training to offset these kinds of attitudes and prevent the stress and burnout that promote them.

Training should also equip employees with the ability to work with children with maltreatment histories. Caring for abused and neglected children is difficult and training is a way to support caregivers and reduce punitive, potentially abusive, responses to symptomatic behavior. Hobbs, Hobbs, and Wynne (1999) call for extra provisions for youth who are victims of child sexual abuse. These children are at risk of becoming perpetrators themselves; their behavior may become sexualized and maladjusted. Therefore, to protect other youth in care, employees must understand the processes by which a victim may become an offender and be able to identify warning signs that these youth are a danger to others and themselves. Hobbs, Hobbs, and Wynne (1999) further assert that maltreated youth need to be provided with much more treatment from advanced mental health professionals for their psychological problems.

The training strategy may be extended to youth as well. Though it is the duty of administration, staff, and other adult authorities to protect children in care and custody, the youth themselves can and should play a major part in reducing misconduct. As part of its youth intake process, the Massachusetts DYS has developed an orientation that "is gender-responsive and features information about prevention, self-protection, treatment and counseling" (Pihl-Buckley, 2008, p. 45). The orientation includes information on appropriate verbal and physical relationship boundaries, healthy and unhealthy relationships, how to report sexual misconduct, what to do if sexually assaulted, and the importance of not making intentionally false accusations. A brochure is given to youths that can be personalized with the name of one's clinician and advocate. It stresses to the youth the following: sexual contact with youth or staff is completely prohibited; they cannot consent to sex with staff or peers due to their age and status; the agency takes all allegations seriously; they should report any allegations they hear to staff (even if they do not believe them); staff is responsible for investigating allegations; and they will be held accountable for making intentionally false allegations. Materials include PowerPoint presentations with bulleted talking points that enable staff to discuss misconduct issues with youth in a non-threatening way. The orientation package also mentions the DYS's five basic rules of conduct (updated to reflect PREA mandates) that are also posted in all programs (Pihl-Buckley, 2008).

It is also important for upper administrators to receive continued training, especially if they are to become better able to hire good staff. Skinner (2003) mentions that prior to participating in the selection of managers for two new residential youth facilities, senior managers participated in a half-day seminar on safer selection while operational managers who served as hiring process assessors attended a three-day training program. Skinner (2003) found the involvement of Human Resource Managers in the seminar to be important, suggesting that operational managers and human resource managers should work together more in improving the hiring processes.

The responsibility for providing effective training for youth workers extends beyond the agency. Agencies desire to provide extensive training but most lack the resources, namely money, needed to provide it. Cuts in governmental funding at the local, state, and federal levels have forced agencies to cut employee development programs to preserve other essential programs and services. Without better funding, agencies will not be able to provide the kind of training that reduces employee misconduct and other problems (Roush, 2008).

5.1.4 Supervision

Juvenile facilities house offenders and victims, and often youth are both. Residential youth facilities increase victimization risk by placing motivated offenders and attractive targets for abuse in close proximity to one another, unless steps are taken to neutralize this threat. Children's rights to protection indeed include protection from other children. Strategies designed to protect children from maltreatment by professionals do not necessarily protect them from peers (Barter, 1997). Therefore, specific strategies for protecting youth from each other are also needed. Without them, programs may be engaging in program or system maltreatment. Frontline staff spend the most time with youth and are thus the most likely to encounter peer victimization. However, they are also more likely to lack the training and qualifications to properly deal with peer victimization. To prevent and respond to peer victimization, staff must be active leaders; they must have the ability and legitimate authority, as supported by management, to set boundaries for peer behavior (Barter, 1997).

Employees must understand the victimization threats that exist in youth care institutions. Roush (2008, p. 34) states: "The protection of vulnerable youths from sexual violence at the hands of staff or at the hands of other predatory youths include a set of circumstances that are unique to juvenile victims and their emotional development." To provide better protection, staff should be educated in juvenile victimology and recognize current threats such as bullying and bias-motivated offending or "hate crimes." Also, frontline staff should be provided with support from psychiatric and psychological service specialist staff in supervising and caring for disturbed and violent youth with victimization histories (Warner, 1992, cited in Kendrick, 1998).

Increased supervision of youth by staff is helpful in reducing peer violence to the extent that staff members are capable of providing proper supervision (Peterson-Badali & Koegl, 2002). Roush (2008) identifies the need to train staff to properly supervise youth and prevent youth-on-youth misconduct, such as violence directed toward lesbian, gay, bisexual, transgender, and questioning (LGBTQ) youth. To prevent bullying in child care institutions, Browne and Falshaw (1996, pp. 126–127) recommend the following: For the bully, "assess factors that elicit bullying behaviour in the individual" and "develop specific social skills and anger management through a personal programme of treatment." For the victim, "assess factors in the individual that elicit bullying by others" and "develop specific social skills through a personal programme of treatments." For the institution, "assess methods of staff management and control of young people with challenging behaviour" and "reduce use of threats, intimidation and humiliation by staff in managing young people and promote reward systems to control behaviour." Hobbs, Hobbs, and Wynne (1999) also point out that youth must be intensely supervised during contact visits to protect them from abuse by family members.

Institutional security is needed to prevent both employee and youth misconduct but is not a sufficient strategy in itself. Security can even potentially increase misconduct. Security is largely achieved by depriving youth of autonomy over their daily lives, which tends to bring about a great deal of psychological distress. Though necessary for the safety of everyone, institutional control is largely coercive in nature. Some youth respond to such distress with violent behavior toward peers or staff. MacDonald (1999) studied samples of California Youth Authority (CYA) male parolees. He found that individual youth characteristics prior to incarceration (represented by official criminal history) significantly increased the odds of violent institutional misconduct (officially recorded assaults toward peers or staff) occurring, but so too did level of institutional security (CYA classification of limited, moderate, medium, and close), which also increased the odds of drug misconduct occurring. Further, MacDonald's (1999) multicollinearity test did not suggest that the level of security was simply a reflection of the criminal histories of the youth being housed. Limiting youth behavior through tight monitoring and controls is not enough to eliminate institutional misconduct. As the training issues covered earlier suggest, employees must also engage in a variety of therapeutic activities that protect the physical and psychological well-being of youth.

To summarize, strategies for preventing professional misconduct against youth may be outlined as follows.

Policies and Procedures
- Clearly State Prohibited Behaviors (comprehensively and specifically) and Disciplinary Actions
- Incorporate Established Professional Code of Ethics
- Recognize Need to Protect Youth in Collective Bargaining (if union)
- Apply Policies and Procedures Thoroughly and Consistently in Daily Practice
- Continuously Re-Evaluate and Revise Policies and Procedures for Effectiveness

Hiring
- Use Rigorously Planned Procedures, Including Models Developed and Tested Over Time
- Always Carry Out Procedures Formally and Thoroughly in Each Phase
- Use Several Interviews (individual and group), Tests, and Exercises to Evaluate Fit
- Always Conduct Thorough Reference and Background Checks
- Attract and Retain Better Employees with Incentives and Support

Training
- Include Both Pre-Service and In-Service
- Focus on Maintaining Proper Boundaries with Youth
- Focus on Child Development, Victimology, and Behavior Management
- Clearly Identify Appropriate Vs. Inappropriate Interactions with Youth
- Teach Employees Stress Management Techniques

Supervision
- Staff Must Always be On the Lookout for Potential Peer Victimization
- Training Should Also Include How to Supervise Offenders and Victims
- Avoid Level of Security and Deprivation that Worsens Violent Youth Behavior

5.2 DETECTION

Employees should receive proper training in recognizing and reporting misconduct (Asbridge, 2007). It is important that administration and staff are able to recognize the "red flags" (events, actions, activities, or circumstances) indicating that professional misconduct against youth may be taking place and that an investigation or inquiry is needed (Roush, 2008). Considering mandatory reporting statutes and other legal and civil matters, Roush (2008) recommends that administrators become better trained in conducting investigations of alleged institutional child abuse, and that administrators and staff understand the importance of documentation to investigation outcomes. If an employee is to be dismissed over charges of abuse, then documentation should support and justify such action, especially if the agency wishes the action to be independent from criminal prosecution and avoid a lawsuit by the dismissed employee. Hobbs, Hobbs, and Wynne (1999) recommend that youth care systems develop better policies and procedures for investigating allegations of abuse. They also recommend that youth in placement receive thorough pediatric health care checks that may detect signs of maltreatment, and that maltreated youth remain on a child protection register during placement (so that health workers are aware of the maltreatment). Further, Roush (2008) believes that every institutional policy and procedure manual should require dismissal and possible criminal prosecution for any employee who fails to report known or suspected incidences of child sexual abuse.

5.2.1 Reporting

Children must have someone to turn to when their safety is threatened. One basic strategy to detect maltreatment is to "listen to the children." Histories of youth in correctional placement often include lying and other deceptive or manipulative behaviors, but professionals must resist the urge to automatically dismiss youths' complaints on this basis. In fact, being "unbelievable" may make one an attractive target of abuse. Also, some evidence suggests that placed children who formally report maltreatment are usually telling the truth (Lyon, 1997). Organizational culture must make it easy enough for children to complain (clear and satisfying procedures), assure children that they will not face reprisal for complaining, and even draw from youths' complaints to improve services (Kendrick, 1998). Multiple mechanisms must exist for reporting and investigating threats to youth in placements. For example Freundlich, Avery, and Padgett (2007) suggest that youth be provided with a toll-free 24-hour hotline to call when their safety has been threatened or violated, and statements by youth should be included in standard critical reporting and reviewing systems that assess incidents in which youth safety is an issue. Freundlich et al. (2007, p. 185) also state:

> Specific procedures to respond to documented safety issues are needed to ensure that affected youth are protected, that the future safety of affected youth as well as other youth in the congregate care setting is assured, and that action is taken against agencies that do not comply with safety requirements (through corrective action plans and/or adverse decisions regarding the continued contracting with these facilities for services).

To be able to use helplines, youth in residential treatment programs and foster homes must have access to private telephones (Kendrick, 1998).

Youth work is often contextualized by isolation from public view, stressful work conditions, and camaraderie among employees holding the same or similar positions (frontline staff or supervisors for example). Such circumstances may foster an employee subculture that embraces staff vs. youth ("us vs. them") and "don't tell" attitudes, as well as Machiavellian beliefs about controlling problem youth. This type of workplace culture makes it a hostile environment for employees who "want to do the right thing." Thus, employees must also have someone specific to turn to when they come to learn that colleagues have, or may have, maltreated youth (Kendrick, 1998). Youth workers have a formal duty to report suspicions and concerns of maltreatment, but will be reluctant to do so if "whistleblowing" tends to be somehow punished by peers or superiors. They may fear retaliation, even dismissal. Similar to youth, employees must be able to bring their concerns to someone outside of their line management structure and be assured that genuine complaints will not hurt their daily work or long-term careers. Detection is greatly supported by legislation that protects employees who in good faith report institutional child maltreatment (Kendrick, 1998).

As part of a strategy for addressing assault, Asbridge (2007) recommends the following to administrators: First, existing reporting mechanisms should be examined to ensure that youth are provided with multiple methods for reporting victimization by staff, including access to outside investigative bodies unaffiliated with the agency, and that it is documented that youth adequately understand these methods. Second, administrators should frequently talk with staff and youth about matters concerning their well-being, as continued engagement counters a "code of silence" about issues of assault and the belief by youth that nothing will be done to help them. Third, existing internal procedures for investigating juvenile complaints should be critically evaluated to ensure that the agency is fully able to properly investigate and report alleged offenses. Finally, the agency must ensure that procedures are in place to provide appropriate medical care for victims and that all staff members know how to use them.

To provide true protection, youth service organizations and oversight agencies cannot just create opportunities for youth and constituents to make complaints; they must also facilitate youths' utilization of complaints procedures. This begins by providing youth with information on their rights, complaint procedures, and contact information for organizations that can help them. This may include simple measures such as passing out leaflets or booklets and directly assisting youth throughout the process (Lyon, 1997). Utilizing bureaucratic procedures to represent one's interest is a difficult task for an adult, let alone a child. These procedures involve complicated processes which in reality often contain formal and informal obstacles. Children, especially those from low socioeconomic backgrounds, often have little knowledge of their rights and little awareness of available courses of action. Law usually mandates that children in custody are made aware of and understand complaint or grievance procedures, children are encouraged and assisted in using these procedures, and such procedures are independent of the agencies targeted by complaints. Still, in reality, youth may be deterred from reporting maltreatment (Lyon, 1997). One barrier is the uphill battle youth may experience during the complaint process. Fearing the consequences of founded cases of maltreatment, agencies may have lawyers represent their interests in response to complaints. Placed youth, most with low socioeconomic backgrounds, lack the knowledge and financial resources to likewise acquire a lawyer to represent their interests. Because youth lack confidence in "the system," they may be discouraged from even attempting to seek legal representation and go forward with their complaints. Intentional or not, agencies may be able to use legal bullying tactics to conceal cases of child maltreatment. Therefore, youth will at times require legal assistance in making their maltreatment known (Lyon, 1997).

Agencies should have their own mechanisms for resolving youths' complaints in the hopes of eliminating the need to take a complaint further, but should not use internal procedures to prevent youths from making external complaints (Lyon, 1997). Youths must have an independent person to go to with complaints, such as a social worker, children's rights officer, or other advocate. However, if these advocates are affiliated with, even if not directly employed by, the agency targeted by a complaint, it becomes questionable whether or not they can truly represent a youth's interests over that of the agency. Some may not adequately represent children because they lack qualifications such as an understanding of care systems. Youth will often realize this and simply see the advocate as part of the same system responsible for their maltreatment. Those maltreated by professionals who are supposed to do the opposite, protect them, may distrust any social service authority. Further, placed youth may not really have access to outside authorities. Some settings do not provide youth with access to private telephones and agencies may not provide independent persons to receive complaints at all because of financial cost. It is crucial then that youth have unobstructed access to persons whom they can go to with complaints and that they are able to believe that these persons are truly independent of the agencies holding them. One possibility is to select child representatives from separate child advocacy organizations, and ensure that placed youth are made fully aware of and can contact these organizations (Lyon, 1997).

After an assessment of its policies and procedures regarding sexual misconduct, the Massachusetts DYS determined that it could be more clear and consistent with its youth grievance reporting procedures. In response, a more "child friendly" grievance form was created and locked drop boxes were planned to be placed in every facility to provide youths with an easy way to report sexual misconduct when they are not comfortable reporting it to staff. The boxes were to be placed in areas easily accessible to youth, and the forms were to be collected by staff in the chain of command outside of the locations (Pihl-Buckley, 2008).

5.2.2 Investigation

Child advocates or ombudspersons tasked with investigating alleged employee maltreatment of youth must be well-trained, thorough, and objective (Matsushima, 1990). This is especially important when interviewing alleged victims, alleged perpetrators, and witnesses. While the investigator should try to take the perspective of the interviewee, one's role is to dispassionately evaluate evidence in an effort to discover what actually happened—not seek to confirm an initial account. For example, leading questions must be avoided: interviewees should be able to give their accounts in their own words. Interviewing is especially important in marginal cases, as interviews may provide the only evidence as to what happened. In some cases there are no witnesses to an event possibly involving maltreatment; interviewing the alleged victim(s) and perpetrator(s) may be the only path to a judgment. It is essential, then, that staff are trained to look, listen, and be alert during crises, including those being handled by other staff, so they may act as better witnesses if called upon (Matsushima, 1990).

In addition to increased commitment and skill, systematic improvements to investigations are needed. Investigating child maltreatment in institutional settings presents particular difficulties. Investigations of institutional maltreatment differ from investigations of familial maltreatment in that, with the former, authorities are often scrutinizing their own environment—their organizations, related departments or agencies, or peers (Barter, 1999). Independent investigators are usually required by law, but they may still have strong ties to professionals and agencies targeted by accusations of child maltreatment. It is doubtful that investigators will always pursue "their own kind" with the same diligence they use when investigating subordinate outsiders, namely low socioeconomic status families.

Barter (1999) interviewed 41 child protection investigators in England and Wales about investigations they conducted between 1994 and 1996. Most cases investigated involved serious allegations of physical or sexual abuse by professionals in residential children's homes. Participants identified problems that could interfere with independent investigation. Though the investigators worked for a separate child advocacy agency (National Society for the Prevention of Cruelty to Children), the agency's service-level agreements with youth service authorities made some worried about "rocking the boat too much" within an investigation. None recalled any actual threats made by the commissioning authorities, however. Other uncomfortable situations included investigating within the team's own geographical area, investigating professionals in related fields, especially those whom they knew, and having previous contact with and knowledge about a facility, which could affect their objectivity. Several investigators were worried that the workers they investigate will discuss the investigations with colleagues outside their facilities, which might result in harm to the investigator's relationships with other professionals. Some reported difficulty in resuming working relationships with professionals they investigated, regardless of outcome. Other problems were identified. Some investigators found the remit and scope of investigations too restrictive, preventing an evaluation of the role of parties beyond individual staff, such as management. Several believed that the local authority did not give enough support to the youth alleging abuse. Several also found post-substantiation procedures, such as feedback on investigation findings and decisions regarding investigators' suggestions for policy and practice changes, to be weak (Barter, 1999).

Barter (1999) offered suggestions for policy and practice, tentatively based upon the exploratory study. Even if an external agency conducts investigations, national and local protocols are needed to ensure complete independence. These protocols should include measures to address the conflicts of interest that may be inherent in service-level contracts between agencies. Investigators should be geographically separated from the facilities and individuals under investigation. (Some study participants reported less conflict when investigating out of their own geographical area.) Also, investigations should be used to evaluate the broad support youth are supposed to receive for reporting maltreatment. Finally, post-substantiation procedures should be clarified and formalized. Investigators and youth should both be informed of investigation outcomes. In fact, another element of independence may be added in this post-substantiation phase. Investigation reports may be presented to a third party oversight or advocacy agency which would then be responsible for evaluating recommendations and monitoring any resulting changes to policy or practice (Barter, 1999).

In 2004, the Arizona Department of Juvenile Corrections (ADJC) began implementing structural changes intended to create a culture of safety for both youth and staff (Dempsey, 2007). The department's Internal Affairs Unit was reorganized into an Inspections and Investigations Division. The division has a clear chain of command to the ADJC Director, which helps ensure timely notification of significant issues and events. Also, a new reporting mechanism was developed that allows anyone to report serious staff misconduct directly to the director (Dempsey, 2007). Other agencies are also trying to increase reporting of misconduct by providing alternative mechanisms for reporting. For example, the Massachusetts DYS sexual misconduct policy allows staff to confidentially report incidents to the agency's General Counsel's Office (Pihl-Buckley, 2008).

Dempsey (2007, p. 88) described the new ADJC division's inspections unit:

> ...the Inspections Unit was charged with providing the director and his leadership team, comprised of agency division directors and managers, with a "baseline" of where the agency stood regarding daily operations and compliance with policy and procedure. This information was determined through random audits, formal audits, leadership-directed inspections and safety inspections.

The new inspection process allowed for the identification of deficiencies, inconsistencies, and other problems regarding rules and procedures. In response, a Policy and Procedure Unit was developed that collaborated with internal stakeholders to match policies and procedures with best practices. The Inspections Unit evolved into a system of self-analysis and improvement that both identifies problems and requires action plans to solve them. These plans could include training and changes to policies, structures, and processes. Ideally, the Inspections Unit and audited stakeholder will agree upon a specific, planned completion date. The unit then conducts follow-up inspections to ensure that these plans are implemented. In 2007, inspectors referred to as "institutional coordinators" were assigned to each of the agency's facilities:

> They perform quality assurance functions and support facility leadership in developing continuous improvement activities. Their primary focus is to initially monitor "core" areas, such as separation/exclusion, use of force, youth on youth assaults, suicide prevention and grievances. (p. 88)

It is the intention of the new inspection process to empower employees to participate in quality assurance, thereby increasing their confidence that best practices are being used, as well as establishing pride and ownership in continuous improvement (Dempsey, 2007).

The division's Investigation Unit is in charge of investigating incidents occurring within ADJC jurisdiction (Dempsey, 2007). Increasing pay to attract better investigators and enhancing training to include best investigative practices were among the steps taken to improve these investigations. Also, the unit was divided into subunits: Criminal Investigation and Professional Standards. The Criminal Investigation Unit was staffed with state-certified police officers to investigate criminal allegations. The benefits of such an in-house unit are that the investigators will have a better understanding of the agency's mission and culture and that investigations can be tailored to "the unique environment and victimology present in a juvenile correctional system" (Dempsey, 2007, p. 89). Further, prosecution was aided by educating local prosecutors in resident victimology as well as in the nuances of cases and their impact upon the safe operation of secure care facilities. As with inspections, investigative policies and procedures were developed to reflect best practices and clearly identify all of the steps and expectations involved in conducting child abuse investigations. Policies included multidisciplinary investigation protocols for county attorneys, child protective services, law enforcement, and medical and mental health caregivers (Dempsey, 2007).

The Professional Standards subunit of ADJC Investigations was staffed with experienced correctional officers trained to investigate alleged staff misconduct. Relationships with ADJC legal staff, the youth rights ombudsperson, and the attorney general liaison were improved to increase the transparency of investigations, and a specific conduct policy was written to identify consequences for unacceptable employee behavior. Also, an automated electronic case management system was created that routes all alleged offenses to the Investigations Unit and investigation summaries to ADJC leadership. This system has the advantages of immediate routing, clear supervisory oversight and quality control of investigations, and increased transparency (Dempsey, 2007).

Finally, four other measures were added to the Investigation Unit to increase safety. A narcotic detection canine unit consisting of two specially trained and certified correctional officers was created to prevent drugs from entering facilities, and a homeland security/intelligence officer position was added to improve disaster readiness. Two measures improved the quality of employees and others with youth contact. An investigator trained to conduct thorough background checks of prospective employees was permanently assigned, and a database was developed for tracking background investigations for contractors, providers, interns, volunteers, and visitors (Dempsey, 2007).

Better detection does not guarantee better protection of youth. For example, improved complaints procedures do not necessarily lead to better protection as authorities may frequently decide that complaints are invalid or outside of their responsibility to handle, or they may fail to develop concrete protective actions in response to valid complaints (Lyon, 1997). Therefore, improvements must also be made to intervention—and future prevention—responses to professional misconduct committed against youth.

To summarize, strategies for detecting professional misconduct against youth may be outlined as follows.

Reporting
- Develop Thorough Internal Reporting Mechanisms
- Train Management and Staff in Recognizing and Reporting Misconduct
- Use Disciplinary Action against Employees Who Do Not Report Misconduct
- Protect "Whistleblowers"

- Detect Maltreatment of Youth through Health Screening
- Facilitate Youth Reporting, Including to External Sources
- Provide Youth with Legal Aid
- Avoid Adversarial Responses to Youth Who Make Complaints

Investigation
- Develop Thorough Internal Investigation Protocols
- Fully Cooperate With and Support External Investigation Laws and Procedures
- Investigators Must be Well-Trained, Thorough, and Objective
- Develop Investigation Procedures That are Truly Independent
- Use Results of Investigations to Improve Anti-Misconduct Policies and Procedures

Intervention
Bloom (1993) points out that an agency has three responsibilities when a residential staff member is accused of committing sexual abuse. The first is to protect the safety and well-being of the child. The child must be supported emotionally and protected from possible retribution by staff or peers, and extra efforts should be made to respond to particularly vulnerable children. Bloom (1993) makes six specific recommendations here. First, it is important to believe that sexual abuse by staff can happen. It may be difficult to believe that a child care worker would be capable of such an offense, especially at an agency with a fine reputation, but it does happen. Unfortunately, hiring processes are not always able to detect such individuals, especially if there are flaws in hiring. Second, allegations must be taken seriously. Regardless of initial impression, the interviewer must be thorough and listen to the child carefully and empathetically. Third, because sexual abuse is a serious charge, it is necessary to suspend the employee with pay during the initial investigation. Doing so not only protects the child and agency from potential further harm, it also protects the employee from allegations of interfering with the investigation. Fourth, the agency should reach out to the child's family. While also ethically correct, doing so will potentially neutralize adversarial relationships. Fifth, the agency must prevent retribution by staff members or peers. The accused may be well liked by the children and other staff members, who may have a tendency to act antagonistically toward the alleged victim. Sixth, the agency should flood the child with support. The child will be in need of the full range of crisis intervention services available to victims of

sexual assault, and though in some cases the allegations will turn out to be false, the agency must side with the child until that time.

The second responsibility is to support the staff. Accusations of sexual abuse make it difficult to maintain a favorable work environment. Bloom (1993) makes eight recommendations here. First, like alleged victims, alleged abusers must be interviewed fairly and objectively, allowing them to tell their stories. Second, it is important that the agency conducts itself in a fair and professional manner by treating the alleged abuser with respect and dignity. Third, the agency should explain to the alleged abuser that the suspension is not a finding of guilt but necessary to meet the agency's primary duty to ensure the safety of the child. Fourth, as a part of fair treatment, the alleged abuser's wage and benefit status should be maintained until the time that the person may have to be discharged. Similarly, fifth, the agency should explain and support the alleged abuser's due process rights. Sixth, an informational meeting of all residential employees must be convened to assure them that the agency is still in charge and to calm any anxieties they may have about the agency's functioning. Seventh, the staff must be prepared to deal with the anticipated reactions of the children as they may resent the victim, be angry and distrustful toward staff, or re-experience their own past abuse. Eighth, the staff must be kept informed as events happen, but the agency must keep the focus on supporting the children and prevent a preoccupation with the situation that interferes with the duty to provide treatment.

The third responsibility is to maintain the organization, which is in large part done by meeting the prior two responsibilities. At stake is the organization's reputation and ability to offer effective treatment. Bloom (1993) makes six more recommendations here. First, an agency must resist any compulsion to "deny, cover up, and defend." These responses contribute to underreporting and can worsen the damage caused by incidents of abuse. A better defensive strategy is to be forthright, unambiguous, and communicative in managing the impact of the abuse. Similarly, second, "shareholders"—those who have a stake in the operations of the agency (e.g. board of directors, major referral sources, executive staff, clients, community at large)—must be informed. Third, the circumstances of the abuse will be better managed if the agency places one clearly visible and accessible senior administrator in charge. Fourth, the agency should anticipate and prepare for legal action prior to receiving threats, including contacting the agency's attorney and insurance company. Fifth, the agency should prepare for media coverage and direct all communication to media outlets through the managing administrator. Sixth, to begin preventing future incidents, it is important that the agency is thoroughly examined to identify and eliminate institutional factors that facilitate abusive behavior; for example, those that may exist in hiring, orientation and training, and supervision practices as well as policies.

As part of its protocol development, the Massachusetts DYS collaborated with other state agencies and organizations in responding to cases of sexual misconduct victimization (Pihl-Buckley, 2008). The agency held discussions with representatives from the state Department of Health and rape crisis centers along with sexual assault nurse examiners (SANE) about issues concerning best care for youth sexually assaulted while in DYS custody. These included how to safely and securely transport allegedly victimized youth and "the importance of having a staff member with whom the youth is comfortable—preferably one of the same gender—present during the rape kit collection to support the youth and provide security" (Pihl-Buckley, 2008, p. 45). SANE nurses educated staff on evidence collection and preservation, including rape kit collection, and rape crisis counselors covered specific victim issues such as sensitivity toward the distress that victims experience as a result of being asked to repeat the details of an assault. DYS went so far as to develop protocols for transporting victimized youth to specified SANE hospitals to improve evidence collection and follow-up care (Pihl-Buckley, 2008).

To summarize, an outline of Bloom's (1993) three responsibilities is helpful here.

Protect the Safety and Well-Being of the Child
- Protect the Child from Further Harm, Including Retaliation by Peers or Staff
- Provide the Child with Emotional Support and All Needed Victim Services
- Suspend the Accused During the Investigation (if a serious charge)
- Work Cooperatively with the Child's Family

Support the Staff
- Treat the Accused Fairly and with Dignity, Respecting Due Process Rights

- Convene an Informational Staff Meeting to Handle Concerns Over a Case
- Prepare Staff to Deal with Resentment on the Part of the Child's Peers
- Keep Staff Informed as the Case Develops

Maintain the Organization
- Be Forthright and Avoid Concealing Incidents, While Being Prepared Legally
- Inform Stakeholders of the Situation
- Place One Administrator in Charge of Managing and Discussing the Case
- Re-Examine Policies and Procedures to Prevent Future Abuses

5.3 GENERAL ANTI-MISCONDUCT POLICIES AND PRACTICES

Some policies and practices apply to prevention, detection, and intervention. To begin, staff on youth maltreatment may be more likely to occur during early morning and late afternoon to evening hours. Thus, Blatt (1992) suggests that agencies consider split shifts or flexible schedules for more highly trained professional staff, as well as ensuring adequate programming during these times. Access to professional staff would reduce the stress placed upon frontline staff, increase the quality of intervention when incidents do occur, and increase the quickness of reporting, which is important for meeting policy mandates (Blatt, 1992).

Davidson-Arad's (2005) findings showed that staff and residents in juvenile correctional facilities each tended to be more aware of the other's misconduct. Possibly, employees may tend to underreport employee misconduct while youth may tend to underreport youth misconduct. Therefore, Davidson-Arad (2005) recommends that interventions and programs designed to reduce violence and abuse in juvenile corrections address differences in staff and youth perceptions in an effort to make each group more aware of the misconduct it commits. This may include staff–youth dialogue in which each group becomes more aware of the other's perceptions. Davidson-Arad (2005) suggests that although staff may disagree with youth's perceptions, having their voices heard by staff will support youth's rehabilitation and youth will benefit from staff perceptions through exposure to a "more normative view of violence" (p. 557).

Davidson-Arad (2005) also found that certain types of staff and resident misconduct tended to occur more in certain types of facilities—more staff abuse in closed facilities for instance—and therefore recommends that interventions and programs be designed with the needs of a particular type of facility in mind. Further, Davidson-Arad (2005) found that staff and youth misconduct took place in girls' facilities nearly as often as in boys' facilities. Therefore, it cannot be assumed that these are minor problems in girls' facilities; programs for girls must also take major steps to prevent, detect, and respond to institutional misconduct.

Protecting children's rights is at the heart of institutional maltreatment prevention, detection, and intervention. Protecting these rights should be a community-coordinated effort, involving not only cooperation with governmental authorities and placing agencies but partnerships with child advocacy organizations as well (Kendrick, 1998). Increased contact with the outer community reduces the social and physical isolation of residential programs. Residents should spend as much time in the community as possible, but the community should also have a presence in residences and programs. Children's rights officers or advocates positioned within the child care agency itself, oversight agencies, or partnering organizations play a large role in promoting safety. These officers provide youth with a voice and can help programs deal with children's complaints and concerns. Partner organizations may include those formed by or for youth in care or formerly in care. These can be very instrumental in promoting support for placed youth, awareness of their needs, and implications for services. Involvement from families and the general community is also important. Anyone visiting a facility is in a position to represent the interests of the youth, and residents with little or no contact with family members should be appointed some kind of independent visitor such as a guardian or befriender (Kendrick, 1998).

Nations should join together in a global effort to eliminate professional misconduct against juveniles. Joining many scholars and advocates worldwide, Acoca (1998) strongly recommends that the United States ratify the United Nations Convention on the Rights of the Child (the U.S. has only signed it) and comply with the Rules for the Protection of Juveniles Deprived of their Liberty and other international agreements establishing protections for children in custody.

Acoca (1998) also recommends that the U.S. Congress pass legislation increasing the power of the Office of Juvenile Justice and Delinquency Prevention to monitor and protect children in custody and legislation requiring the Department of Justice to "design standards that recognize and address in concrete terms the unique circumstances of girls and, where appropriate, their children" (p. 584).

To summarize, general policies for reducing professional misconduct against youth may be outlined as follows.

- Involve Youth as Much as Possible in All Anti-Misconduct Activities
- Have Highly Trained Professional Staff Work During High-Risk Hours
- Design Anti-Misconduct Policies and Procedures to Fit Needs in Girls' Programs
- Design Anti-Misconduct Policies and Procedures to Fit Needs in Closed/Secure Facilities
- Involve the Wider Community in Anti-Misconduct Efforts
- Participate in International Efforts to Protect Children's Rights

5.4 CONCLUSION

This chapter covered several strategies to address professional misconduct against youth, which are outlined at the end of each section. Though difficult, plans to eliminate (or at least greatly reduce) misconduct must include several policies, procedures, and practices aimed at improving prevention, detection, and intervention. An approach that uses only a few strategies will likely fail to achieve significant reductions in misconduct, as it will only potentially alleviate a few of the causes of misconduct. Prevention is of utmost importance, of course, but when misconduct against youth unfortunately does occur, better detection and intervention will promote justice, help heal victims, and contribute to the prevention of future incidents.

CHAPTER 6

The Next Step

Studies have provided insights into the nature, extent, and factors of professional misconduct against juveniles in correctional treatment settings, as well as solutions to the problem. Professional misconduct against youth varies widely in type and seriousness. Categories include sexual misconduct, nonsexual abuse, neglect, property offenses, duplicity, and unprofessionalism (poor role modeling). The little research conducted suggests that misconduct occurs frequently enough to constitute a major problem. The literature also proposes causes and risk factors existing at individual offender, organizational, and institutional levels as well as victim characteristic risk factors. Finally, several prevention, detection, and intervention strategies are offered as solutions to the problem. However, there remains much to be learned.

6.1 SUGGESTIONS FOR FURTHER STUDY

The literature is severely lacking in studies analyzing the problem through sociological perspectives. Professional misconduct against youth is a systemic problem. Thus, "bad apple theory" serves as a very incomplete basis for explaining and reducing misconduct. Recognizing that misconduct is not simply the result of individual defects in character and personality but also of facility- and agency-wide cultural and structural factors is a good first step in understanding that extra-individual factors increase misconduct. However, stopping at the organizational level is still an overly reductionist approach to explaining and reducing misconduct. A macro-sociological perspective is needed to understand how larger social-structural factors (e.g. governmental and economic) and cultural factors (e.g. public beliefs about child-raising) operating at the community, state, and national levels serve as facilitating contexts for personal, interpersonal, and micro-organizational factors increasing misconduct. Formal and informal organizational cultures, for example, do not occur in a vacuum. Stress brought about by lack of public and political moral support, lack of material resources for treatment, low pay and benefits, and dangerous environments can promote pessimistic beliefs and attitudes and adversarial relationships among staff, administrators, and youth. Larger social, economic, and cultural forces, then, can foster negative organizational cultures that inhibit rather than promote efforts to reduce misconduct. Also, more study needs to be directed at behavior by powerful individuals that constitutes professional misconduct against youth. As with other forms of offending, studies tend to focus on the behavior of lower status, less powerful individuals—in this case, frontline staff—and tends to ignore elite deviance which can have far-reaching damaging effects.

Much more empirical research is also needed. To begin, more data are needed regarding the extent of professional misconduct against youth. The current body of published research does not provide a clear picture of the magnitude of the problem. National surveys such as those conducted by the Bureau of Justice Statistics (BJS), as required by the Prison Rape Elimination Act (PREA), on sexual assault in correctional facilities would be valuable, especially if they collected data on multiple types of misconduct. More local, state, or regional studies are also needed. The literature contains but a few of these studies, most of which are rather dated. These could include employee self-report surveys. Because of the controversial nature of the behavior, respondents will be reluctant to divulge their own acts of misconduct. However, they may be willing to anonymously report attitudes and beliefs consistent with the behaviors. Studies could use the vignette approach taken by Horwath (2000) to study residential youth workers' judgments on the acceptability of misconduct under certain circumstances.

A sense of the magnitude of the problem may also be gained through more studies examining employee and youth perceptions of misconduct that takes place in their settings. Though subjective, this approach may detect more misconduct that is undetected by official reports and self-reported deviance. As Davidson-Arad (2005) points out, both employee and youth perceptions are important, and more studies should comparatively examine both. Youth and employees have different views, experiences, interpretations, and motives that shape their perceptions of misconduct occurring in their environments, which may yield different advantages and disadvantages of their respective self-reports. Though very imperfect, the combination of the two viewpoints provides a fuller picture of the problem compared to one alone. Examining both also allows for some assessment of how aware employees are of the problems faced by children in their care (Davidson-Arad, 2005).

The limited availability of empirical information on professional misconduct against youth is mostly descriptive. More research is needed to identify the correlates and potential causes of the problem within explanatory theoretical frameworks. For policies and practices to be effective, they must address a larger set of accurately identified factors. Policies and practices based on anecdotal evidence, intuition, poor or very limited research, or simply beliefs and values will not be very effective. Policymakers and practitioners are currently quite aware of several factors that increase the occurrence of misconduct. However, there are likely more factors, especially those beyond the organizational level (i.e. public opinions on juvenile treatment, local educational indicators, and regional economic indicators), that affect the occurrence of misconduct. Also, while it may already be known that certain factors increase misconduct, their relative impacts are unknown. For example, just how much does improper screening contribute to rates of misconduct? Does proper screening reject only serious criminal offenders, or does it also reject other at-risk persons without noticeable criminal propensities (those more capable of exercising poor judgment than anti-social behavior)? In general, serious violent offending constitutes a minority of incidents of crime. Thus, if proper screening only excludes serious offenders from working with youth, then improper screening can only account for a small portion of incidents of misconduct—though of course they may cause the most harm. The practical implication here is that agencies must do much more than screen applicants to prevent misconduct. With this in mind, more evaluative research is needed to test the impact of efforts to reduce misconduct. Several articles describe policies, procedures, and practices that plausibly reduce misconduct but few/none empirically test their effectiveness.

Future research should also explore correlation among different types of misconduct. If different misbehaviors are part of a behavioral complex, studying the specific types of misconduct separately makes them look like relatively small, unrelated matters. A typology framework improves the study of misconduct by tying together behaviors that share qualities, causes, and consequences, and by giving a fuller view of the extent of and solutions to the problem. Such analyses would provide much-needed insight into the nature of professional misconduct against youth and serve as a beginning to examining the broader extent of the problem. Further, since girls in custody face specific challenges, more research is needed on how different types of maltreatment vary according to gender (Acoca, 1998).

Research and literature should also address settings outside of secure and residential facilities. While perhaps less likely, professional misconduct could conceivably occur in juvenile probations, day treatment programs, and other fully community-based programs. While youth do not reside at the sites of these programs, thereby reducing the potential for hidden behavior, they still rely upon adult authority, sometimes in physical environments that are somewhat secluded from the outer community (e.g. day treatment buildings). Therefore, the potential for misconduct in non-residential settings does exist. The author could find no articles published on professional misconduct against youth in these settings.

Finally, global/comparative perspectives on the problem are needed. Institutional maltreatment of youth is a violation of international human rights (Acoca, 1998). Just as professional misconduct against youth in correctional treatment settings is a global problem, the paucity of research on the issue also extends globally. The three studies reviewed earlier—Attar-Schwartz (2011), Davidson-Arad (2005) (and Davidson-Arad & Golan, 2007), and Kiessl and Würger (2002)—are among the few outside of North America that can be found in the literature. Cultural and social institutional differences across countries determine local experiences with the problem, yet similarities may also exist that create general patterns of causes and consequences. More global/comparative scholarship on professional misconduct against youth would not only reveal these similarities and differences but may also suggest ways that agencies in different countries can learn from one another in responding to the problem.

6.2 TAKING ACTION

Kendrick (1998) points out that providing safe, caring environments for children involves not only actions in organizational management, planning, and daily practice, but also in politics and policymaking at local and national levels. Needed is a "holistic and integrated approach" that accounts for the daily experiences of youth in placements and how they are linked to 1) the broader organizational contexts (including policy) in which care is provided, 2) relationships between different professions and agencies, and 3) social, economic, and legislative processes which underpin the provision of child care and protection (Kendrick, 1998). Further, it is essential that governments apply international children's rights standards in their oversight of youth correctional programs and facilities (Acoca, 1998).

As argued earlier, the causes of professional misconduct against youth are rooted in the political, economic, and cultural structure of society as a whole. One solution to the problem, then, is a very difficult one that agency administrators and other authorities cannot carry out alone. A larger social movement is needed whereby the public 1) comes to believe in the potential of juvenile corrections to help youth and in the importance of protecting youth with problem behaviors and 2) responds with the willingness to prioritize resources needed to create effective juvenile corrections. This involves not only a personal dedication to funding correctional and rehabilitative services, but also the demand that political and economic leaders re-allocate resources toward them. In addition to advocacy groups and organizations, politicians, bureaucratic leaders, business owners and corporate leaders, and other community leaders may use their influence to make youth work a higher priority (i.e. allocate more resources toward juvenile offender treatment). The public in general is needed to carry out this macro-social solution. Any person can help out by supporting reputable child advocacy organizations—those which pass careful scrutiny—with actions such as donations and volunteering. Also helpful are supporting governmental child welfare agencies through cooperation and political action, such as informing representatives of one's wishes to maintain such agencies.

In sum, and to conclude, action to eliminate professional misconduct against juveniles in correctional treatment settings must be taken at multiple levels. At the individual level, professionals become less likely to engage in and more likely to detect misconduct through better hiring practices and training, and empowered youth become more likely to report victimization. At the organizational level, policies, procedures, staffing practices, and management structures aimed at better prevention, detection, and intervention foster a workplace culture that strongly resists misconduct. At the community level, youth, staff, and management would all benefit from working relationships with other local organizations as well as concerned citizens. However, these efforts rely on an increase of resources available at the societal level. Thus, more public education, public support, collective action, and political reform are needed to effectively address the problem of professional misconduct against youth.

REFERENCES

Acoca, L. (1998). Outside/inside: The violation of American girls at home, on the streets, and in the juvenile justice system. *Crime & Delinquency, 44*(4), 561–589.

Asbridge, C. (2007). Sexual assault in juvenile corrections: A preventable tragedy. *Corrections Today, 69*(5), 80–85.

Attar-Schwartz, S. (2011). Maltreatment by staff in residential care facilities: The adolescents' perspectives. *Social Service Review, 85*(4), 635–664.

Barter, C. (1997). Who's to blame: Conceptualising institutional abuse by children. *Early Child Development and Care, 133*, 101–114.

Barter, C. (1999). Practitioners' experiences and perceptions of investigating allegations of institutional abuse. *Child Abuse Review, 8*, 392–404.

Beck, A. J., Adams, D. B., & Guerino, P. (2008). Prison Rape Elimination Act of 2003: Sexual violence reported by juvenile correctional authorities, 2005–06. *Bureau of Justice Statistics Special Report* (NCJ 215337). U. S. Department of Justice Office of Justice Programs.

Beck, A. J., Cantor, D., Hartge, J., & Smith, T. (2013). Sexual victimization in juvenile facilities reported by youth, 2012. *Bureau of Justice Statistics Special Report* (NCJ 241708). U. S. Department of Justice Office of Justice Programs.

Beck, A. J., Harrison, P. M., & Guerino, P. (2010). Sexual victimization in juvenile facilities reported by youth, 2008–09. *Bureau of Justice Statistics Special Report* (NCJ 228416). U.S. Department of Justice Office of Justice Programs.

Beck, A. J. & Hughes, T. A. (2005). Prison Rape Elimination Act of 2003: Sexual violence reported by correctional authorities, 2004. *Bureau of Justice Statistics Special Report* (NCJ 210333). U. S. Department of Justice Office of Justice Programs.

Blatt, E. R. (1992). Factors associated with child abuse and neglect in residential care settings. *Children and Youth Services Review, 14*, 493–517.

Bloom, R. B. (1993). When staff members sexually abuse children in residential care. *Residential Treatment for Children & Youth, 11*(2), 89–106.

Browne, K., & Falshaw, L. (1996). Factors related to bullying in secure accommodation. *Child Abuse Review, 5*, 123–127.

Davidson, J. C. (2004). Where do we draw the lines: Professional relationship boundaries and child and youth care practitioners. *Journal of Child and Youth Care Work, 19*, 31–42.

Davidson-Arad, B. (2005). Observed violence, abuse, and risk behaviors in juvenile correctional facilities: Comparison of inmate and staff reports. *Children and Youth Services Review, 27*, 547–559.

Davidson-Arad, B., & Golan, M. (2007). Victimization of juveniles in out-of-home placement: Juvenile correctional facilities. *British Journal of Social Work, 37*, 1007–1025.

Dempsey, J. (2007). Culture change ensures safety for staff and youths in juvenile corrections. *Corrections Today, 69*(4), 88–89.

Freundlich, M., Avery, R. J., & Padgett, D. (2007). Care or scare: The safety of youth in congregate care in New York City. *Child Abuse & Neglect, 31*, 173–186.

Groze, V. (1990). An exploratory investigation into institutional mistreatment. *Children and Youth Services Review, 12*, 229–241.

Hobbs, G. F., Hobbs, C. J., & Wynne, J. M. (1999). Abuse of children in foster and residential care. *Child Abuse & Neglect, 23*(12), 1239–1252.

Horwath, J. (2000). Childcare with gloves on: Protecting children and young people in residential care. *British Journal of Social Work, 30*, 179–191.

Kay, H., Kendrick, A., Stevens, I., & Davidson, J. (2007). Safer recruitment? Protecting children, improving practice in residential child care. *Child Abuse Review, 16*, 223–236.

Kendrick, A. (1998). In their best interest? Protecting children from abuse in residential and foster care. *International Journal of Child & Family Welfare, 2*, 169–185.

Kiessl, H., & Würger, M. (2002). Victimization of incarcerated children and juveniles in South Africa. *International Review of Victimology, 9*, 299–329.

Lerman, P. (1994). Child protection and out-of-home care: System reforms and regulating placements. In G. B. Melron, & F. D. Barry (Eds.), *Protecting children from abuse and neglect* (pp. 353–437). The Guilford Press.

Lyon, C. M. (1997). Children abused within the care system. In N. Parton (Ed.), *Child protection and family support: Tensions, contradictions and possibilities* (pp. 126–145). New York: Routledge.

MacDonald, J. M. (1999). Violence and drug use in juvenile institutions. *Journal of Criminal Justice, 27*(1), 33–44.

Matsushima, J. (1990). Interviewing for alleged abuse in the residential treatment center. *Child Welfare, 69*(4), 321–331.

Peterson-Badali, M., & Koegl, C. K. (2002). Juveniles' experiences of incarceration: The role of correctional staff in peer violence. *Journal of Criminal Justice, 30*, 41–49.

Pihl-Buckley, H. (2008). Tailoring the prison rape act to a juvenile setting. *Corrections Today, 70* (1), 44–47.

Powers, J. L., Mooney, A., & Nunno, M. (1990). Institutional abuse: A review of the literature. *Journal of Child and Youth Care, 4*(6), 81–95.

Pringle, K. (1993). Child sexual abuse perpetrated by welfare personnel and the problem of men. *Critical Social Policy, 12*, 4–19.

Rosenthal, J. A., Motz, J. K., Edmonson, D. A., & Groze, V. (1991). A descriptive study of abuse and neglect in out-of-home placement. *Child Abuse & Neglect, 15*, 249–260.

Roush, D. W. (2008). Staff sexual misconduct in juvenile justice facilities: Implications for work force training. *Corrections Today, 70*(1), 32–34.

Sedlack, A. J., McPherson, K. S., & Basena, M. (2013). Nature and risk of victimization: Findings from the survey of youth in residential placement. *Juvenile Justice Bulletin*. U. S. Department of Justice Office of Justice Programs, Office of Juvenile Justice and Delinquency Prevention.

Skinner, K. (2003). Safer staff selection. *Social Work Now, 25*(September), 31–36.

Ward, A. (1999). 'Residential staff should not touch children': Can we really look after children in this way? In A. Hardwick, & J. Woodhead (Eds.), *Loving, hating and survival: A handbook for all who work with troubled children and young people* (pp. 327–339). Aldershot, UK: Ashgate.